THE REAL DEAL

THE LIFE, DEATH
AND
RESURRECTION
OF
ROBERT CLAYBURN NASH

Jim Bryson

The Real Deal

The Life, Death and Resurrection of

Robert Clayburn Nash

By Jim Bryson

Scripture quotations are taken from the New International Version, © 1973, 1978, 1984, 2011 by Biblica, Inc. Used by permission of Zondervan.

ISBN: 9798692501493

Published by Spring Mill Publishing

Sharpsburg, Maryland 21782 USA

Graphics by Amani Hanson (NoBoxez@Yahoo.com)

DEDICATION

To my good friend, Clay Nash, without whom none of this would be real. Indeed, I have my doubts about some of it, but hey... it's the South, now isn't it?

To my wife, Jacqueline, who pledged herself to my side and has never left it, although sometimes she's wished otherwise in my striving to learn what it is to be a man.

To my children, who have taken the brunt of my faults even as I tried to impart the hard-won gold of my struggles and experiences. May you learn to refine the ore from the dross.

To Lady Jane, my first Bible teacher, who took in a 17-year-old runaway and introduced him to the blessings of Christ and the depths of his Spirit.

And to God. It's been a wild ride and showing no signs of slowing. I love living life with you, Father — the life we share. Thank you.

ACKNOWLEDGMENTS

Thank you to all my test readers: friends, family, neighbors and perfect strangers whom I happened to meet on city buses or in restaurants or on hiking trails and the conversation inevitably came around to the fact that I was a writer and would they like to read a chapter or two and give me comments or better yet, can I read something to you?

Most notably (but not limited to): My sister Jess, my daughter Nora, my granddaughter Samantha, my friends Katie Tinsley, Karey Kimmel, Brad Herman, Jesse Dunlap, Bryan Nicolosi, David Byers, Sean Sell, Julia Roat, Jesse Dunlap and of course, Niki Borggren, my bartender, who, upon hearing of my sketchy plans for retirement from engineering, offered this sage advice: "I'll tell what you're *not* going to do. You're *not* going to spend every day in here with me."

TABLE OF CONTENTS

FOREWORD

BY DUTCH SHEETS

I make known the end from the beginning,
from ancient times, what is still to come.
I say, "My purpose will stand,
and I will do all that I please."

Isaiah 46:10

THE BIBLE IS RICH WITH STORIES of unlikely heroes of faith —
unlikely, not because of gift-deficiencies, but due to
character flaws and sin.

- Jacob was once a lying, conniving swindler.
- Moses, for forty years of his life, was an exiled, has-
  been ruler.
- Rahab has prostitution in her biography.
- David succumbed to adultery and murder.
- Paul, before becoming an apostle, was a
  murderous persecutor of Christians.

And that's the short list. Yet, all of these people, along
with many other seemingly disqualified humans, became
heroes of the Christian faith. Some from this list are
actually foreparents of Christ in His human lineage;
others wrote portions of the Bible!

Without dispute, if there is anyone who has the right
to be cynical of us humans, it's God. He has certainly seen

it all. Yet, far from being cynical, Yahweh remains our greatest fan and responds to us with undying faith. And when one of us wayward humans finally returns to Him, it makes His day. There is no greater joy in Heaven than when a broken person is transformed and Holy Spirit ushers her or him into God's family. Scripture actually says Heaven throws a party (my interpretation of the angels rejoicing and of the prodigal's welcome home celebration) when one sinner comes to Jesus. And the only picture painted in Scripture of our Heavenly Father actually running (what a picture!) is when a father ran to embrace his returning prodigal son. What a great Dad we have!

God's love, however, is just the beginning. When He finds a willing person, the Almighty is extremely confident in His ability to reshape and transform them. (He's also been known to make them willing.) From his vantage point of seeing the end from the beginning, God is able to see us flawed humans, not as ugly pieces of coal, but as brilliant, multifaceted diamonds. Where we see a messed-up life, even a complete failure, God is already seeing flashes of light. Ezekiel tells us when we see dry bones, God sees an army of great warriors.

Clay Nash is one of those diamonds and a General in God's army. Early in his journey, referring to Clay as a diamond—even "in the rough"— would have been pretty gracious. Like so many of God's pre-mined treasures, He was just an ugly chunk of coal—on the outside, that is. But aren't you glad God looks inward to our hidden potential, and forward in time, seeing us as His prized gems? I'm forever grateful that He didn't wait until after Simon's Pentecost transformation to rename him Peter, "the Rock." "I know you'll be cursing and denying me soon, Peter, but I've already seen your subsequent transformation, and in my mind, you already are what you'll one day be."

Who can really fathom the greatness of our God?

One of the great words in the New Testament for purpose and destiny is the Greek word prothesis. Our English word "thesis" is derived from this word. The prefix pro means "pre" or "before." In referencing our destiny, therefore, the use of prothesis means that God wrote a thesis about us before we were born! But the word tells us even more. We also get our English word "prosthesis" from this Greek word. A prosthesis restores purpose to something lost. In His use of this word, Holy Spirit is assuring us that when Satan or life's circumstances endeavor to cut us off from our purpose, God, who sees and declares the end from the beginning, already has a plan to restore it!

What was written in Clay Nash's thesis? The heart of a true husband and father, the loyalty of a covenant friend, an accurate prophet, a wise apostle. In The Real Deal, you'll see his transformation. You'll be impressed and amazed at the Master Potter's grace and skill, and thoroughly convinced that God still finds purest gold in miry clay—no pun intended.

I'm proud to call Clay Nash my friend.

Enjoy!

INTRODUCTION

THESE ARE STORIES FROM THE LIFE of my friend, Clay Nash, known to many as Apostle Clay Nash. I have been captivated by his stories since working on his first book, *Activating the Prophetic*. Possessed of an admiration for the culture of the deep South, and having grown up with neither culture nor father, it was a blessing for me to be in the flow of this great man whose stories never seem to end.

When we wrote his second book, *Relational Authority-Authentic Leadership*, I took Clay's stories to a new level, letting them teach things that plain narrative could not adequately convey.

Such is the nature of the Gospel.

When we look at the Bible — that collection of sixty-six books written by more than forty authors over thousands of years — we can't miss the abundance of storytelling. Truth, shared through actual events, is absorbed by the reader's imagination. Thus, it conveys a reality greater than any teaching.

When God wants us to understand his power to deliver, for example, he shows us the Israelites fleeing the Egyptian army through the Sinai desert. And when faced with the impassible barrier of the Red Sea while the mobs of newly freed slaves are openly mutinous and declaring their allegiance to the taskmasters of Egypt, God shows us his faithfulness through Moses' declaration: *Stand fast and see the salvation of your God!* As Moses strikes the sea with his shepherd's rod and the waters part, our hearts open too, allowing God's Spirit to enter our deserts before closing in on our enemies.

This can't be taught; it can only be experienced. Show first. Explain later. Isn't that what Jesus did?

In heralding a new covenant with mankind, Almighty God sent his Son to show, lead and teach. It is no coincidence that the New Testament opens with five books of stories — four gospels and the book of Acts — before the letter-writing Apostle Paul ever dulled a quill. These records demonstrate the power of God before he tries to teach it.

The stories in this book are true, mostly. I took the main elements — a truck (yeah, there are a few trucks), a bottle (keeping it real), a fistfight or two (Clay wins most of them), some rough language, a fiercely loyal family, a merciful God and an abundance of love, mercy and just enough guilt to bring conviction — and wove them into stories about a new purpose in Christ. The dialog and situations are close to the real events, but of course, they aren't an exact replica. Nobody had video back then. (That's probably a good thing.) Instead, the stories flow from the heart and impart the spirit of the events, telling of a life authenticated by God. Clay Nash would rather disturb you with the truth than pacify you with fairytales. The power is in the truth.

Naturally, most of the names and settings have been altered to shield the innocent, hide the guilty and safeguard those who are still in witness protection. In fact, we hid the details so well that if you think you recognize yourself, that just confirms that you're wrong and any resemblance is sheer coincidence.

Deep calls unto deep.

The message of a story is in the telling, uncovering in the heart of the listener a corollary, a truth suspected all along, a song they heard somewhere before but can only hum a few bars.

Let these pages bring you into a deeper awareness of the Father's love and forbearance for all of his children:

for those in his arms
for those reaching for his arms
for those running from his arms.

May God bless you all.

Jim, you sound like a drunk Yankee

trying to talk Southern.

- Clay Nash

THE KILLING

1970

IT WAS MID-SEPTEMBER, White River forest, deep in the Arkansas night. Crickets and cicadas joined in a throbbing chorus as I eased the truck through the grassy woodlands. Headlights off, I was navigating by starlight on this moonless night, scanning the darkness for signs of others and seeing nothing, no lights, no tracks, no one at all. I kept the windows down, feigning a broken air conditioner, listening for sounds through the sweltering heat, dry grass and twigs crackling beneath my tires.

I glanced over at the older man sitting next to me. Billy was at least thirty-eight—nearly twice my age. I could smell his sour breath, the stale beer from his filthy shirt, the staggering odor of a chronically unwashed body. His skin bore the marks of a lifetime exposed to the elements, ruddy and dry, unshaven, open sores festering, hands rough and dirty, nails black with grease.

We'd been working all day, drinking most of the night. My shirt stuck to my chest. My mind ached. We were both sweating, but me more so. I fought to keep my nerves from showing, my breathing even.

Just keep him drinking.

"Get you another one, Bill. Half a case to go."

"Don't mind if I do, son."

Billy smiled giddily, lifted the lid and plunged his tattooed arm into the metal box. I kept the truck idling in gear, gliding through the path I'd scoped out days before, right after I'd found out what he'd done. Billy pulled his hand from the ice box, stuck the cold can against my neck and laughed. I pushed it away.

"You gonna drink it or play with it?"

We were getting near the spot where I figured he'd need to get out. He giggled and made the familiar gush of a pull-top being ripped off. I watched as he tilted his head back and poured the cold beer down his throat, spilling half on his shirt. Silently, I counted my steps, searching for mistakes. I couldn't find any. We were getting close.

"Clay, you know what they say about beer?"

"What do they say, Billy?"

"You don't buy beer; you rent it!"

"You got that right, Billy. Right over there OK?"

"Ah hell, son, anywhere's good.

I stopped the truck near a deep crater left by the root ball of a fallen tree. Billy slid from the wet vinyl seat and staggered away. As I studied the back of his head, the hate I'd been suppressing flooded my mind like a black-water pond. Billy was a drifter who'd come into town every year or so, mess around with some odd jobs, and always seemed to be leaving about the time some woman started crying. People were used to his coming and going. No one would miss him. Everyone would assume he'd moved on again and would be back someday.

"Ah, this feels good," laughed Billy as he splattered the dry ground.

I carefully reached behind the seat to the pistol I'd stowed this afternoon. Six bullets in the cylinder. At this range, I would only need one. It didn't need to kill him, just lay him out.

As I took aim, I began to shake. I figured it was just the heat, or maybe the salt stinging my eyes. I'd grown up hunting — I knew my way around firearms — but never felt like this before.

Come on, Clay, remember what he did. One quick shot, drag him into the hole, and the varmints will do the rest.

I'd never killed a man before, but if ever one needed a bullet in the back, it was this man.

I fought to steady my hands and tried to ease the trigger into place. *Don't jerk, squeeze,* Dad always taught me. Angry and resolute, I tried again. But my hands shook more and soon were uncontrollable. It felt strange. It was fear, but not a fear of getting caught. I didn't care about that. My family controlled everything that happened in five counties. No sheriff was ever elected in these parts without getting the Nash approval first. I always knew they could get me out of any trouble I got into.

No, this was a fear I couldn't place. I'd fought six men at a time, faced men bigger than me. I'd been in knife fights. I'd lied to enraged husbands about their cheating wives hiding in my house. I'd been robbed and had gone to collect with interest. But never in my life had I ever felt like this. It was as if something greater than me was calling me to account in a courtroom I'd never seen. I hadn't done the deed yet, but it was as if I did. And I couldn't face it. I was about to rob a man of his life just like he'd robbed me, but suddenly I was the one on trial. My whole body shook. I was paralyzed, crying inside, scared beyond belief and ready to bolt from this place if only I could figure out how to outrun whatever it was. I had come here to hold another man accountable. Instead, I was facing accountability.

No one had ever told me about a Holy God who adjudicated the affairs of man, but I knew one thing: I couldn't kill this man. Not tonight; not any night. I was done. My young life as a murderer had come and went.

Billy, with his back to me, was finishing up and none the wiser. He climbed back in the cab and reached for his next beer, looked at me and said, "Damn, son! You look like you seen a ghost."

Hate him? I couldn't tell. But I knew deep inside that something bigger than me would deal with the likes of him. Right now, it was dealing with me. I knew it wasn't about Billy. It never was. I'd never see him again, nor did I want to.

I'd gone to kill a man that night. It would take years before I understood who that man really was.

MOM AND DAD

1947

IT WAS A BRIGHT OCTOBER DAY as Robert (Bob) Dean Nash, surrounded by his eleven brothers and sisters, stared at a coffin suspended over a freshly-dug grave. His mind wasn't on his father, Bill Nash. It wasn't on the heart attack that killed him or the cancer that took his mother eight years earlier—not even on how he was going to get on in life. No, being an orphan didn't bother him, even though he loved his dad. Behind those blue eyes burned the dreams of a thousand schemes and ambitions, the next great idea to try and win. Loss was just the price you paid for winning. Bob was small for his eighteen years, but he dreamed big and worked hard. Work was fun, it was life, the expression of all he was and could be. He gave himself fully to anything he put his mind to. Truth was, he bored easily, so he kept moving from challenge to challenge. Nothing satisfied him for long. There was too much world out there to stay on one half-acre. He and his older brother Roland had a saying: "There's nothing we can't do."

They would spend a lifetime proving it.

On the other side of the grave, among the outside mourners, stood a pretty girl named Dorthy Laverne Bennett, or "Vernie," as her friends called her. She wore a black chiffon dress, white gloves, pearls and a laced hat with a flower atop. She held her hands beneath her modest bosom in a portrait of piety, poised and composed, a perfect picture of sympathy hovering over the freshly churned soil staining her high heel shoes. At first glance, Vernie was the epitome of the southern belle, a peal ringing in remembrance of the antebellum South. Yet under the fine gloves and half-sleeves was another story, one of callouses, cuts and bruises from working in her family's grocery store and part-time at the local drug store. The Bennetts weren't poor, not by any means, but they worked hard to stay afloat. Vernie was no stranger to hauling boxes, stacking shelves and sweeping floors, but late at night after the front lights were extinguished and it was just her and the broom, she flowed to the Blue Danube Waltz playing in her mind, the romance of a working girl whose birth had come a century too late.

Vernie was at the funeral to honor the man she knew from the drug store, a regular who provided a respite to the tedium of her daily life. Bill Nash was an affable gentleman and fond of conversation, especially over a soda with a pretty girl on long summer afternoons. Bill never met a stranger. That was life in small-town Arkansas in the '40s.

"We are here to honor William Nash. He was a... good man. Known by many, honored by most, loved by..."

Ah, get on with it, will ya? thought Bob.

Pastor Glasgow was a retired farmer who'd gone broke when drought killed his final beet crop. A rotund man, his black vestments fought a losing battle to restrain his girth. Sweat flowed from his neck, crested over his gut and found its way to his knees in dark stains of fervent devotion.

Bob, growing bored, scanned the familiar landscape — the farms and fields and forests on distant hills, the roads north to Jonesboro, east to Memphis, and west to Little Rock.

Money to be made everywhere.

As the burial ritual floated through his mind, he began to troll deeper waters.

How many acres does it take to grow hay for a farmer and his family? Figure planting and harvest. Why... that one man might only need a hay baler for two weeks at a time. What would he do with it the rest of the time? Let it rot? But if three men were to share a baler — no, rent it — well then, the maintenance business alone would...

He stopped. He'd found something. What was it? A pretty girl in a netted hat standing on the other side of the burial hole was glancing back at him shyly. *How long have I been staring at her?* It didn't matter. Bob Nash possessed the kind of looks that could get a woman in love with him before she knew his name.

Bob knew the game. He smiled back, his boyish charm melting any concerns she might have had about this starry-eyed stranger who was constantly searching for an angle to play.

I know her from somewhere. Didn't she hang around the store? Yeah, wait. That's Vernie! Nah... can't be. Why, she was just... Well, hell if it ain't. Damn, they grow up fast. Put 'em in a dress, a little make up. My God, girl!

Vernie tried to stay reserved. A young woman couldn't be too forward in rural Arkansas. After all, hadn't she had her share of suitors since coming of age? None ever stuck, though, but at this moment, it wasn't easy holding herself in. The death of one man was offering her the life of another, for on the far side of the grave stood the most handsome man she'd ever seen.

Pastor Glasgow was running out of breath like a locomotive pulling into a depot. Bob wanted to leap across the coffin and make his introduction. *What's a grave when you can fly?* Then his mind flashed to his carpentry tools stashed in the truck, of his plans to return to West Texas and work the booming housing market just as soon as he buried his father. He remembered the girls and the saloons and the Texas swing music playing from every gin-joint on every dusty street in Amarillo.

And just as quickly, he dismissed it all with one more look at Vernie Bennett.

His brother Roland tapped him on the shoulder, breaking his reverie. Bob looked around. The preacher was gone. The coffin was in the ground. Folks were shaking hands and paying their respects and making plans for dinner.

"We gotta get back to the house, Bob. We got a lot of work to do before you run off."

"What are you worried about?" said Bob, searching the milling crowd for Vernie.

"Bob, didn't you see who didn't show?" said Roland.

The realization hit him hard.

"Oh, hell. No!"

Eight years prior, after his first wife died, Bill Nash had remarried a widow, Elizabeth Martin, who had several young children of her own. It was a lively homelife but she never took to Bill's children. They learned the hard way the meaning of "redheaded stepchild."

After my Grandfather's funeral, Bob and Roland and the rest of the siblings rushed back to the farm to discover what had become of Elizabeth, not sure what they'd find.

Of course, Roland, the oldest, was out and married by now, and Bob — somewhere in the middle of the pack — was on his own, but a fair number of young Nashes were still on the farm and would need help sorting things out. When it was apparent that their stepmother had skipped the wake, Roland hoped for the best. *She was overcome with grief; she stayed home to mind her kids; she was busy putting all his affairs in order; she was cooking for the guests.* Anything but what they feared... and found.

The house had been cleared out. No sign of Elizabeth or her offspring. The painted wood floor was bare but for shadows in dust where the furniture had been. The wallpapered walls bore dark squares matching the pictures that had hung there for decades. The cupboards were bare. The blankets and linens were gone, probably to wrap the dishes. While Bill Nash's children were burying their father, his wife — their stepmother — stole everything they had left in life. They would never see her again.

Good riddance.

Within a year of that turbulent wake, Vernie and Bob tied the knot in true Southern fashion. They married, he built her a house, and they moved in and commenced housekeeping, at which point, conceivably, I came to be.

Funny how someone can rob the obvious treasure and miss what is most precious. My family always enjoyed nice things: good land, productive livestock, sturdy houses, cars and boats, but we valued the means of production above all — the business sense and work ethic that made those things possible. See, you could steal a Nash's car — though you wouldn't get far; we were everywhere — but you could never steal the enterprise that made that car possible.

Grandpa's house had been cleaned out, but he left behind a farm-equipment business. Dad and Roland took over the Minneapolis Moline dealership in Wheatley, Arkansas. Possessed of entrepreneurial spirits, always looking for a fresh start, a new challenge, an angle to play on an underperforming situation, the Nash brothers infused new life into a staid business by building relationships with the local famers.

There's nothing we can't do.

Theirs was the union of unfettered capitalism and boundless ambition in an age when a handshake was a deal, your word was your bond, your office was a pickup truck and the communion of the saints rode jauntily in a hip flask beside the thirty-eight special nestled safely in the glovebox.

Dad recognized early that business was done outside of the store walls. He spent his days driving to farms, siding up to the farmers, sharing stories and good whiskey while leaning against worn fences, getting to know the men behind the machines—their struggles, their needs, their dreams, even their women.

People buy from people.

The deal would be the last business of the day.

It would not be long before I entered this fraternity of fiery entrepreneurs. Everything I wanted in life was being lived out before me. For my future, my destiny, my purpose in life, I looked no further than Dad. I never felt whole apart from him. We communicated effortlessly, at times even wordlessly. Growing up in the bosom of my father, we were like paint on a wall. I was possessed of his business spirit, his affinity for relationships, his taste for the tools of sales—long days, late nights, hard drinking and cut-rate deals. I took it all in. I would make my first half-million by age eighteen. And it wouldn't be long before I was faced with choices no teenager should ever have to make.

So much that I see now that I didn't see then. A boy loves his dad as God. And when you worship someone, you don't see the good from the bad. Good is whatever they are, and bad is whatever comes against them.

I was good.

But... I'm getting ahead of myself.

A BIRTH

1953

On the day I was born
The nurses all gathered 'round
And they gazed in wide wonder
At the joy they had found.

George Thorogood

IT ALL STARTED ON MAY 4TH, 1953, in Little Rock, Arkansas. As the nurses of St. Vincent's hospital gathered on that warm spring morning, the first-born child of Dorthy (Vernie) Laverne and Robert (Bob) Dean Nash burst from the womb. After a swat on my rosy wet cheeks, kicking and screaming, I looked around and said, "Hey! Why all the lights?"

At least, I'd like to think it was that way. Truth be told, my entrance into this world was unremarkable except for the fact that *every* child is a gift of God, the future of mankind, a miracle of human seed, the completion of the circle of life.

Lying on Mother's belly, smelling of blood and disinfectant, I must have looked quite the sight. Owing to the Cherokee in our bloodline, I had a tan as if I'd been in the sun all week. My head was covered with loose, black curls and I had a lungful of air to herald my arrival.

"Another Nash Rambler just rolled off the assembly line," Dad said proudly, slapping the doctor's back as my war cry terrorized the delivery room.

He named me Robert Clayburn Nash after his oldest brother, my uncle Roland Clayburn Nash. Being one of thirteen siblings gave him an appreciation for the mass production of Nashes. "This world needs a lot of things, but what it needs more than anything is more Nashes." Or so he said. I'm convinced that he loved Mom, although I am equally convinced that marrying her was for the children they could have together. I was the first installment in what he hoped would be a long line of progeny.

The same boundless ambition that fostered my family's business acumen must have reached my DNA, because I was born with a truckload of it. From the time I could hold a toy or shake a tool, I was ripping them asunder, smashing them against the floor to see what made them tick—or stop ticking. I stress-tested rattles against crib railings, dismantled toys and rebuilt them. I even tore the sides off my mini-tractor to see how the pedals made the rear wheels go around. Strange, they didn't go around after that.

I had an insatiable curiosity and a drive to match. I couldn't stop. I never sat still. My mind chased answers like a pack of hounds running down a buck. Soon as I had one thing figured out, I had three more questions—more toys, more schemes, more machines, more…more…more.

Dad was proud of his first son. Mom was relieved that I'd come out healthy. I was well cared for by my babysitter—an African American lady, Mary Thornton, who loved me as her own. I had it all.

Five years into it, however, I got my first taste of what can happen to the best-laid plans.

It was August, which in Arkansas means *hot*. No, not Yankee hot. I mean Arkansas hot. A staggering wall of steam. No need to press your shirt. Sweat that saves you the trouble of getting wet. A deep breath burns your lungs. You finally understand "slow." Songbirds forget their tunes. Weary dogs take refuge in the shade of tall buildings and pedestrians step over them. Fighting spouses drop their guards and offer terms of peace. It's that hot.

To get a break from the withering days, Dad hooked the boat to the GMC pickup truck and we headed to Clarendon Beach, a sandbar on the White River. It was nature's way of reminding us that it didn't hate us, it just got a bit riled from time to time. My family was devoted water people. Dad was an expert water skier. Mom looked great in a bathing suit. And I floated like a rock.

Toward evening, with the sun's light long and red, I sat at the edge of the lapping water digging in the sand with my plastic shovel and starfish bucket. I was probably hunting crawdads, sifting for clams and arrowheads, or planning how much concrete slurry I'd need in the footers of the Nash Memorial Bridge I was going to build across the river. From a far-off galaxy, I heard my mother's voice.

"Clay, honey. We're packing up. Time to go home, sugar. Let's go now. Come on."

Of course, this was not in my plans. Fortunately, I had the drill down pat. Head down, I kept working in the sand. There was a lot to do before I could leave. Concrete trucks don't always run on time, and if the slump tests failed, that State man would be all over us. *What whiskey did he favor?*

Mom would get over it; she always did.

Her voice came sharper.

"Robert Clayburn Nash! Now! We're gonna leave you behind if you don't mind. Let's go!"

Using my full name meant I had one more callout before she'd bring in the reinforcements, so I kept working. *What do you mean, it's gonna rain? It ain't gonna rain. Pour that slurry and let's get on with it!*

Well, I'd figured wrong. As I would do throughout my tumultuous childhood, I miscalculated the stakes in this game of brinkmanship.

"Bob. Get your son! He's not minding me...as usual. I swear, you're the only person he'll listen to. You really gotta have a talk with him."

I was in real trouble now. Mom made a lot of noise but Dad took action, although I'm hard pressed to remember a time when he had to wail me. He could give me a look that was worse than anything his hands could do.

The game was rapidly coming to a close, so I collected my treasures, registered my soil samples, cut my workforce loose for the day, opened a tab for them at the local beer joint and started to stand. I must have lost my footing in the wet sand, however, because I was still there after my brain said "move." Things were tightening up and seconds mattered. I marshalled my muscles and commanded them to get me on my feet, but my legs must have fallen asleep while was digging.

The tone of her voice scared me.

"Bob, I've had it. One of us is going to have to give him a lesson on minding his Mom! This is ridiculous."

"Is that so, boy?" Dad said as he tied the boat on the trailer. "We'll have to see about that."

"Mom, I'm coming," I cried in panic.

I leaned into the wet sand and tried to push myself up with my arms, flapping around like a beached fish, the sand filling the edges of my bathing suit, anything to show that I was mobilizing to get there fast. But I wasn't moving!

I screamed at my disobedient legs: "Move, doggone you! You're gonna get us in trouble with Dad."

Yet instead of the familiar pins and needles of waking limbs, I felt nothing. No pain, no blood, no hot or cold. A new fear crept up my spine, something I hadn't counted on. I knew I was in deep trouble with more than Dad, if such a thing were possible.

I was shaking and crying as Mom stalked toward me in full regalia, a fierce-eyed Dad at her heels. I flailed harder, crying loudly, the sand sticking to my wet face. Anything to show I was trying. Maybe I could fly away before those angry hands fell from the sky to flail my backside—and for what? What did I do now?

Quaking now, confusion flooding my mind, I was a five-year-old in quicksand, sinking rapidly and recoiling from the only arms that could lift him from this morass.

My parents stopped dead in their tracks. I made the most of my last chance.

"Mom! Dad! I can't make my legs work. They won't go. Dad...?"

My parents rushed me to Doc Walker in Brinkley, Arkansas. In a sterile, cold examining room, he checked me over, realized this was beyond his country-doctor skills, and dispatched me straight to Labonner Hospital in Memphis, Tennessee.

"Clay is a very sick little boy, Mr. Nash. He has encephalitis" was the somber pronouncement of Doctor Eledorf, a lab-coated physician surrounded by diplomas testifying that everything we heard within these hallowed walls would be the undisputable truth, so said Vanderbilt University.

"What the hell is that, Doc?" asked Dad.

"Sleeping sickness, Mr. Nash. It's common in horses and birds. It's carried from infected animals to humans through mosquitoes. It causes the brain to swell and produces the kind of paralysis that Clay is experiencing."

"But he's gonna be OK, right Doc?" pleaded Mom.

"There is a chance, Ma'am, but it's slim. I'm sorry, but this disease is almost always terminal. The best we can do is palliative care.

"Palliative *what*?" asked Dad.

"We keep him comfortable, Mister Nash. Until...until the end."

"Oh my heavens!' cried. Mom. "There was Jackson's sister. Didn't she have that, Bob? I think she died from it. Oh my God!"

Dad lowered his head. His young son's life had just begun and the clock was ticking. Time on earth was fading rapidly.

Dr. Eledorf admitted me to the hospital to run more tests, but these only confirmed his diagnosis. There was no hope. My brain would continue to swell, the paralysis would worsen, and I would die in a matter of months. Lay my body in a little white coffin with gold trim, read some pithy words about God needing one more angel and drop me in the ground forever.

My parents begged the doctor to try something... anything. So, a spinal tap was performed. I don't recall the exact medical purpose, but I do recall vividly the agony of a needle the size of a pitchfork tine being shoved up my spine without anesthesia. The head nurse assisting the procedure was in tears. Dr. Eledorf made Dad leave the room before he started. They locked the door.

When abject torture failed, they tried electro-shock therapy—sticking a thousand needles into my leg muscles and turning on the juice. While I wasn't happy being transformed into a high-voltage pin cushion, anything was better than being trussed like a pig on a spit. But the shocking treatment did nothing to stimulate my floundering limbs. The only lasting effect of this treatment was a phobia of needles that I carry to this day. My wife, Susan, does not even knit. I buy my sweaters from Wal-Mart.

With no hope for recovery, Dr. Eledorf could only reassure my parents that he would keep me comfortable as possible as I passed from this world to the next. *Palliative care*, they had said. But for some reason, I heard *pallet care*, conjuring up images of being carried around on a wooden pallet like Dad used for heavy parts at the dealership. *Maybe they'd bury me on one of those?*

Regardless, the verdict was in. If I was a puppy, they'd gas me to sleep. If I was a colt, they'd shoot me. If I was a GMC diesel, they'd sell me to the scrapyard. Still, I'd have taken the bullet over another pitchfork any day.

In the weeks that followed, they kept me in a drab hospital room the color of puke. I figured that was so nobody'd notice when you lost your lunch. From the moment I had been admitted, Mom wouldn't leave my side. The nurses wheeled in a squeaky cot and she took up residence with me in the bowels of my suffering.

Dad spent a lot of time away. He had work to do, and watching his boy die didn't make him feel productive. Better to channel his grief into something — anything — that he could control. He was grieving the only way he knew.

It was about that time that my parents brought my babysitter, Mary Thornton, to see me at the hospital. Mary was a strong Christian woman who couldn't care less what medical science said. With my mother hovering over me, Mary pronounced her judgment:

"Miss Nash, the Lord told me that Mister Clay is gonna be just fine. He's gonna grow up and preach the gospel all over the world."

"Mary, that's nice. But I don't think you understand the gravity of the situation here. Clay has a very serious disease, and he's not getting any better."

"Miss Nash, I only know what the Lord told me, and I'm telling you, Mister Clay is gonna be just fine. He's gonna preach the gospel."

The tears in my mom's eyes told another story. Southern culture in those days required that we bore politely the fables of well-meaning folk. The golden rule was *never be rude.* No matter what. Rudeness was a term reserved for Yankees, the lowest of all lifeforms. Mary didn't look like us, but she was family, and she loved me, even if she was misguided.

My parents continued to steel themselves for the worst while peppering the medical staff for anything that would alleviate my suffering. I was still their son, Clay, whom they loved, but their expectation for me to carry the family name had not included a granite marker on a verdant hillside with flowers and a teddy bear left on my birthdays.

At least... not yet.

One morning, about 2 a.m., as mom slept in her cot that wheezed with every breath she took, I found myself wide awake with a voracious appetite. I hit my button and a nurse fetched something she thought I could keep down—grape juice and crackers. As she laid them on my tray, she remarked offhandedly: "This is like the Lord's supper, huh?"

I was less interested in the body and blood of Christ and more concerned for my ravenous stomach. I devoured the simple meal and fell back asleep. In the morning, feeling better for the first time since my ill-fated construction project on the river, I slid my legs over the side of the iron hospital bed and walked to the bathroom, just a little kid going to pee like Mary Thornton had taught me. As I emerged from the toilet, my mother was sitting on the edge of her cot. Something wasn't right.

What was wrong with Mom?

I think it was her screaming loud enough to wake the dead.

"CLAY, BABY. WHAT ARE YOU DOING?"

"Why? Am I in trouble again?"

"No, Baby. You're not in trouble." She was crying now. "How'd you do that?"

"I went to the potty, Mom. I washed my hands. See?"

"Oh my God, Clay! Walk to me, Baby!"

I reached my Mom and she touched me gently, her hands shaking. Suddenly they were in the air. She was jumping and crying: "Praise Jesus! Praise the Lord! Hallelujah!"

By now, the nurses were in the room wondering what all shouting was about. They saw me and began yelling: "It's a miracle; Thank you, God; Go find Doc Eledorf!"

I had just taken my first steps in months, just as Mary Thornton had prophesized.

"Can we go home now?" I asked. "I want to play with my truck."

"We'll go home, Baby. We sure will. Oh God. Oh my God. What happened to you, Clay? What made you walk?"

"I had to pee, Mom."

In those days, people didn't get healed. Sure, healing ministries showed up sporadically throughout the South, but my people tended to discount these as charlatans — and most of them were. We were salt of the earth. We were good to you as long as you were good to us. We believed in an honest day's work, a wild night's fun and no coke in our whiskey. We gave no quarter to fairy stories or religious fantasy. Cash on the table was what mattered — tactile evidence.

I will always remember the day my mom acted like a Pentecostal — a conversion lasting about a week. The joyous reunion of my parents lasted a bit longer, but not by much. It had a greater impact on me than just restoring my legs. It completely changed how I interacted with the world. Despite the joy of my healing, I required months of therapy to restore what the illness had destroyed. This meant weeks in the clinic on a stationary bicycle redeveloping the nerves and muscles ravaged by the insidious attack.

All that time ailing and recovering affected my personality. To this day, I hate being sick and sitting still. Further, all those hours on machines enhanced my innate technical aptitude. I developed a deep, uncanny ability with all things mechanical. I would eventually become the best diesel mechanic for miles around, parlaying my skills into a successful trucking company with tractor trailers that could outrun anything but a State Trooper's radio.

Back in the first grade and nearly recovered, however, a second event occurred with an equally lasting impact on my life. My elementary school teacher, Miss French, insisted that my predilection for left-handedness spelled trouble. For my part, I spelled *trouble* T-E-A-C-H-E-R. But nobody was asking me; I was just a kid.

Well, this expert on child development convinced my parents that I would never develop mentally as long as I remained a southpaw. So, every time I reached with the offending appendage for a pencil, a fork or a crayon, she smacked it out of my left hand with her ever-present ruler. (Thankfully, she never followed me to the restroom.) Finally, to save my bleeding knuckles, I gave up and started doing things her way — the *right* way.

Which explains why, in subsequent testing for personality disposition between right-brain and left-brain preference, I always came out firmly in the middle, to the extent that the testers suspected I was cheating.

Despite the life-long benefits of a balanced mind, I smoldered with resentment at the unnatural switch forced upon me. At the ripe old age of six, the embers of the Nash obstinacy seared deep within me.

Who the hell do they think they are?

It burns to this day.

COMING APART

1965

THE WHIRLWIND ROMANCE of my parent's marriage was unraveling at a pace that neither one would halt, even if they could. Things were coming apart at the seams.

Emerging from the post-war prosperity of my miraculous healing, ages five to twelve found me torn in three directions, the epicenter of an unhealthy trinity. Each member loved me deeply and differently and sought to influence me in their own way. The only question was to whom would I give my allegiance.

As if that was ever in question.

Mom tried to raise me as a nun. Sadly, she was on the losing end of the battle to keep her boy out of trouble. Her boy wanted trouble. He welcomed trouble. Sure, he rarely looked for trouble, but he acted swiftly when it found him. (OK, he might have *invited* it a few times, but just to stay in practice.)

True to my family heritage, I wasn't a bully, but I ended the career of many a bully long before video games replaced mock combat on school playgrounds, backyards and alleys. Even at a young age, my zeal for repaying the oppressor burned violently. I'd thrash the kid who dared pick on the weak. I was never weak.

I would come home sporting black eyes, split lips, bruises and everything else that passed for the badges of courage in rural America. Mom would shriek. Mary would pray. Dad would beam with pride.

"What'd the other guy look like, son?" he'd say. "Did he crawl away or run? I bet he begged you to stop."

"Bob, don't encourage him!" Mom would cry. "Come here, baby. Does this hurt? I told you not to fight. You can't fight in your condition. You've got to be careful, baby. You're still getting well, remember?"

"No, it doesn't hurt. I'm fine, Mom. And I'm not a baby. I'm nine and a half."

"Lord, help that boy be all you're callin' him to be," Mary would pray aloud. "And keep 'im alive 'til then, blessed Lord Jesus."

And he did.

While Mom worked at a western store and Dad ran the farm equipment dealership (and a dozen other ventures), Mary Thornton tended to her pale son. Thank God for Mary Thornton. That woman lived what she believed and she instilled it in me. Her example forged a life-lesson within my soul:

Always preach the gospel, Clay. And when necessary, use words.

It's one thing when an adult adopts a child. It's another thing when that child adopts the adult. My parents had to love me — that's what parents do. But Mary... she *chose* to love me. And in so doing, she conveyed the love of Almighty God who makes us all sons and daughters through adoption, fully grafted into the family of heaven, no seams, nothing to come apart.

My hardworking parents were exhausted. Sadly, instead of pulling together to find what they needed in each other, they sought satisfaction elsewhere — on the road, in the workplace, as supporting characters in some lover's finely-spun fairytale. They found solace among the denizens of the dark, faithless men and women whose emptiness mascaraed as vulnerability, inhabitants of hovels reeking of stale beer and broken luck and restroom stalls covered in scum that even Penicillin was afraid of.

As the battle over my parenting continued, relations between my parents worsened. Dad's drinking grew heavier, as did his womanizing. I don't condemn him. His was a sickness fueled by an innate ability to drop a woman's moral compass straight to her ankles with one disarming look. Dad had these — how can I describe them? — *lady-killer eyes*. Everywhere we went — in business, homes of friends, out of town restaurants, on the street — women hit on him. He took it as a blessing. Today, he'd call it a superpower. He tutored his young son: "Always gotta have something going on the side, son. Life's too short to stay on one half-acre."

It was many years until I understood the truth of this Trojan Horse gift. See, in the male-dominated, competitive culture of our day, mistresses were normal, even expected. But there were rules and a clear understanding of how things should be. Men were expected to have affairs and women were expected to stay chaste. That's logical, isn't it?

The way around this conundrum was the distinction between good women and loose women. The good women kept things to themselves and occasionally to their boyfriends before marriage, and *only* to their husbands after marriage. Among the good women, female fidelity was a paramount virtue, followed closely by the *appearance of fidelity*. The loose women, on the other hand, made themselves freely available to all. It was these that men preyed upon. They were the lowest of the low, tragic souls who traded their bodies for fleeting affections that faded like the scent of cheap lilac water.

It was tragic; I won't lie. But that's how it was.

Dad stayed gone for days. Mom could only tolerate it to a point. Dad eventually stopped coming home altogether. Mom, left alone and still a good-looking woman, did what many lonely women do, and a breakup ensued.

This meant I was faced with a bloody choice. Dad and I were inseparable. We were running businesses together; I was his partner from the age of twelve. We finished each other's sentences. I could read his mind like it was my own. Dad was everything to me. Mom brought me into this life. Mary Thornton showed me eternal life. But it was Dad who gave me daily life.

I wasn't going anywhere without Dad.

Choosing one over the others was the most gut-wrenching thing this boy ever had to do, but there was no choice. Only pain.

Not that I was unfamiliar with pain. Growing up at a time when prayer was allowed in schools but lawyers were not, meant that flawed justice occasionally reigned.

I remember the whooping like it was yesterday. Coach Jenkins, my Junior High School basketball coach, thought he had caught me in some misdeed and he wasn't having any of my panicked explanations.

As his hand gripped my sweaty collar, my choked pleas echoed off the gymnasium walls.

"It wasn't me, Coach."

"Dammit, Clay. I know you did it, boy. You were the only one near the bucket. You thought it'd be funny to take a piss in the mop bucket, didn't you?"

"Coach, no. I didn't."

"Well, that's the first honest thing I've heard you say all morning. It wasn't that funny, was it boy?"

"It was Rodney, Coach. I swear it."

"Oh, you're gonna swear alright, son. You're gonna swear to the deep blue heavens that your momma birthed a spawn from hell, and when we're done, you just might be able to sit in a week or two."

With that, he thrust me over his knee, whipped off his size fourteen sneaker and began to wail me to heights unknown in my brief but turbulent life. It was scathing retribution... but for what? I didn't know. I thought Bob Nash could be vengeful. He was the Angel of Mercy compared to this trusted leader of defenseless boys.

The first swing took the breath out of me. The second threw my hips out of joint. By the third strike, I was no longer thinking. My mind went far, far away, floating through the rafters of the old gym, listening to some poor kid wailing out his innocence and crying for God's mercy.

Coach was just warming up.

From somewhere else, another voice shrieked: "Coach, stop it. It was me. Clay didn't do it. I did it. Coach, please!"

But this was not a moment for intercession.

"Shut up, Rodney. Get the hell outta here unless you want the same."

I limped home that day, expunged of tears and any shred of dignity. Coach Jenkins had broken me. There was nothing left to prove. If no one believed me when I told the truth, what good was truth? As I walked through the door, I was sure to straighten up, however. No telling what would happen if Dad knew. School whoopings had a way of being amplified by well-meaning parents.

Yet for all the pain of Coach Jenkin's beating, it was nothing compared to what Vernie and Bob Nash bestowed on me the day they each decided to go their separate ways.

DIVORCE

DIVORCE IS NEVER EASY. Sure, it appears to be the easy way out—sometimes it's the only way out—but it kills everything it touches. That's the point, though, isn't it? It starts with the death of a romance, then it kills the union of two hearts, and finally, it tries to kill each heart separately. Which is fine if that is what you choose. *Choose life...and live. Or choose death and watch everything you love blow away in the hot wind.*

I say it's fine, but it never is, not really. See, two adults can choose to dissolve their union, split the sheets, cash in their chips, settle up with the house, cut their losses. But a child? He can't split himself in two. He has one heart and it's given to two parents. He's too young to divide himself, and yet, that is exactly what divorce makes him do. So, his heart tears. It rips along the weakest seams and exposes his greatest potential for failure. A divorced child's heart is no longer whole, and it never will be as long as his parents are apart. I'm not sure it can ever be put back together.

The first thing to be destroyed is the shield over a child's heart, the layer protecting what is too precious to be exposed without the love of Mom and Dad together assuring him that everything he feels — primary colors and warm, soft shapes — is true and everlasting.

Torn apart, he screams for something; the heart was never made to be alone. The child grows desperate for someone or something to take up residence and fill the bleeding voids.

I didn't want to hate them. I never did and I never will. They were flawed human beings, and they passed on their flaws to me, along with teeth and hair and a brain and eyes. They gave me their weaknesses and their strengths. Then they forced me to choose: *Lose him or destroy her.*

I was twelve years old, dammit.

No, the hate I felt was *in* me, but it was not *of* me, and that was killing me. When something against our nature rages within us, it destroys us.

I cried into the void and the void answered. I shook my fists and anger strengthened me. I racked my mind and logic validated me. I pleaded for identity and pride stood me.

I would never be alone again. I had all I needed. I could stand. I could make decisions. I could act. As the sky grew darker, a light glowed from within. It was the effervescence of decay, the half-life of a human soul counting down to death. What was meant to sustain my journey to adulthood was consumed for my triage. I grew stronger from a resolute will. The boy who couldn't stand in the sand became the man who could murder the boy.

I would never trust anyone again.

And I would never accept from another what I could get by my own hand.

EMANCIPATION

1965

THE SEASONED EYES OF JUDGE BILL LEE of Monroe County peered down at me from his wooden bench. The seal of the State of Arkansas hung on the wall behind him, and a ragged gavel rested within arm's reach. I thought of the many bad guys it had sent to jail for days, months or years. What high crimes and misdemeanors had been adjudicated here? Who had won and who had swung? Rumor had it that Jesse James was once tried here. But Dad dismissed it.

"Jesse James was never this far east, son."

"What about Dillinger?"

"Nah."

"Baby Face Nelson?"

"No."

"Bill Clinton?"

"He ain't old enough yet, boy. Get back into your story."

The sweltering courtroom predated the Civil War, meaning it was older than the judge but not by much. The oak floor creaked with each step. The ceiling fans churned faithfully but voiced their protest with every rotation: *clink, clink, clink*. A crowd of Nash family onlookers stifled their coughs and struggled to maintain a respectful bearing as the sweat found rivulets beneath their starched collars and underwear. Judge Lee was not known for being tolerant of distractions.

"Now, son, you understand what this means?" said the Judge from his regal roost.

"It means I can work beside my daddy, Your Honor...Sir."

"Yes, son. And it means a little more. Now hear me, son. You'll be on your own. You can sign contracts, make your own decisions and be your own man. But son, you mess up—you step outta line one time—and ain't no momma or daddy gonna bail you out of trouble. Your ass will be mine. You understand me, boy?"

"Yessir, Your Honor Sir."

The judge turned his withering stare to Dad.

"Bob, do you understand that your son will no longer be your responsibility?"

Dad, standing beside me, shifted his weight.

I watched Judge Lee's forehead twitch as Dad mustered the words: "Yessir, Bill, er, Your Honor. I'll still be looking out for the boy. But this will help him. He needs to be on his own. We're partners just as much as we're father and son."

Turning back to me, Judge Lee thundered his final warning:

"Son, if I see you in this courtroom for *anything*, even littering, I promise you won't leave here for a long, long time. None of this 'blue jail for little boys and pink jail for little girls' nonsense. No sir. You'll be tried and sentenced as an adult and pay the full penalty of your deeds. Are we clear?"

I tried to ignore the fleck of white spit hanging on his lower lip. I reckon it'd been there for centuries.

"Yessir. Absolutely clear, Your Honor Sir."

"All right then. By the power vested in me by the people of Monroe County, of the great state of Arkansas, I hereby declare Robert Clayburn Nash an emancipated minor."

CRACK went the gavel.

A sigh came up from the crowd.

"You may now kiss the bride."

"*Sir?*"

"Aww... just joshing with you, son. I love saying that. Congratulations."

A grinning Judge Lee reached down his withered hand and I shook it.

"Thank you, Sir," I said, cracking a smile. "You had me there."

"G'on now. The clerk'll give you your forms to sign. NEXT CASE!"

CRACK!

And with that, I became legally independent of my mother and father at the age of twelve. They say life comes at you fast. Mine just got kicked into high gear.

NAPOLEON

1967

DAD AND I ARE IN BUSINESS, been so since I was five. But now, as an emancipated minor, I can be a full, legal partner.

We are currently running a crop-dusting business that he'd bought from old Mr. Monroe, a notorious drunk who couldn't seem to keep his planes in the air. Well, that's not exactly true. Getting them in the air wasn't the problem. It was getting them down in one piece that was the challenge.

Driving back home, Dad and I go over the next day's plans for Nash Flying Services. It'll be my first day running it on my own. I want to make him proud. I want to see it in his eyes.

Years ago, we'd been running an old steel oil derrick, hoping to get some more oil out of it. Well, the shaking of the engine must have loosened the supports, because it came apart at the base and toppled over, straight at me. Dad had been on the other side and he started screaming "CLAY!" I had ducked and rolled into a ball and it collapsed all around me. In shock, I lay still for a moment, gathering myself and listening to his frantic pleas as he ripped through the broken steel and cable. I never heard him like that before. And I'll never forget his face when he found me alive and unscathed.

"Now remember, son. Four a.m. sharp at the airfield. I'm giving it all to you. I've got other things to tend do. The flight manifest will be on the desk inside the hanger. Make sure the planes are topped off, check the fuel for water, enter the readings into the log books, go over the checklist, and make sure each pilot is ready to go. If he's drunk..."

"...he's gone. Yessir."

"Check the weather reports. Wind no greater than five mph. I don't care what those flyboys say, they ain't taking off..."

"...if the ceiling is lower than 700 feet. Got it, Dad. And if it's calling for rain...

"...they're grounded, son. No questions asked. They ain't gonna like it, but that's how it goes. We pay 'em plenty to fly when they can. They'll get..."

"...the three hours we promised for showing up..."

"...but not a dime more, boy."

"That's right, Dad. Them farmers won't pay..."

"...to have their insecticide washed into the ground an hour later, son."

"Hell no."

"Hell no!"

Tuesday morning, 1 a.m., I'm pouring over log books, mechanical records and the weather report for every county in a five-hundred-mile radius. Four a.m. comes around and I'm looking for my crew. We run three planes and a pilot for each, so we need a ground and maintenance crew. A fourth plane is kept in the hanger for backup.

Four thirty and still no one. The sun is coming up over the tobacco fields. First day running this business and already I'm behind.

Four forty-five and I see dust from the county road leading to our long drive way. Two loader men emerge from a beat-up Chevy truck: Roscoe Smallwood and his brother Elroy. They look surprised to see me.

"Where's Willie and the rest of the crew?" I say, cutting off their pleasantries.

"Where's Bob?" asks Roscoe with a smile a tad too familiar to suite me. He's tall and lanky in his grease-stained flight suit. He takes a step forward and leans over me with a wry smile. Of course, everybody leans over me. Height is never my advantage. But this dog has plenty of fight in him.

"I'm running things here now," I say fiercely, afraid my voice will crack. "Y'all were supposed to be here at four. You're late. That's not gonna fly."

They laugh, throwing me off stride.

"Look, boy," says Roscoe. "You run along and git your daddy, OK? We'll square things with him. Now which plane is mine to load today?"

He grins at my rage, reaches into his front pocket for two Camels, lights them both and hands one to Elroy who pulls a hand out of his tattered jumper to put the smoking stick between his cracked lips.

An alarm goes off inside of me.

"What the heck are you doing?" I scream. "No smoking on the airfield. I've got aviation fuel here. Put those things out. Do it now!"

Elroy smiles at Roscoe and takes a deep drag.

"Young'n sure is excitable today, ain't he?" he says to his brother.

"Aren't you supposed to be in school, boy?" says Roscoe as he exhales moist smoke in my face. "What grade you in, anyway? I got a boy your age. But he knows how to talk to grownups."

"I'm an emancipated minor," I say as my voice cracks.

"Oh, you *'mancipated'* are you?" says Roscoe, imitating my faltering voice. "Well, I got some Ex-Lax in the truck what will help that. You'll be shittin' yer britches in no time. Might even improve your at'tude."

The brothers convulse with hilarity.

I have all I can take.

"Now listen, you two," I scream. "Mouth off one more time and...and... you'll be looking for other planes to load. Yeah...I'll fire you. I can do that, you know. That's right. You hear me? I'll fire you both."

I sound like a hysterical girl. I don't care. This girl is pissed.

The shock buys me a few seconds before the laughter takes hold again. I'm out of cards to play. Fourteen years old and I can't get grown men to listen to me. How am I gonna run this business?

About that time, I see more dust from the county road. A caravan is headed our way. Three trucks pull up and out comes my pilot Willie, the ground crew... and Dad.

It's a calvary bugle, bobbing flags on the horizon, the thunder of horses' hooves. Still, a weight drops into my gut. I should be able to handle these jerks on my own.

"Hey there, Bob," says Roscoe, smiling like he's found a long-lost friend. "We were just saying to your boy here that..."

Strangely, Dad isn't in the mood for talk.

"Smallwoods, what the hell are you doing smoking out here? You know the rules."

The Camels are quickly snuffed out in the turf. I notice how the brothers don't look directly at Dad, even though he and I are just about eye to eye. All heads are flying at a respectful half-mast.

"Listen everybody. You know my son, Clay. Well, y'all are working for him now. I've put him in charge. He's running this operation. If you want to work for a

Nash outfit, you better pay attention to him. He speaks for me, and what he says, goes."

You can hear the dew evaporating on the grass.

"Now, you don't have a problem with that, do ya, boys?"

Dad scans my crew of blackguards, deserters and privateers.

"No, sir."

"Got it, Bob."

"Sorry, son. We didn't mean anything. Just joshing with ya."

"Well, good then," says Dad. "I reckon we won't have any problems. It's all yours, son."

Dad walks away and all eyes are on me.

I shift my weight for emphasis, glance at my clipboard even though I know it by heart — one of the advantages of a photographic memory — and begin to issue orders in my man-voice.

"Roscoe, you got the Willard farm, North and East fields. Two passes. You're loading Alice. She needs to be fueled and ready to go. Check the tail. Linkage is a bit loose. Elroy, you have the University. They said they'd mark it out with orange cones. You're loading Betty. Check her oil before she goes. You know she leaks a little."

An hour later as the third plane, Christine, takes to the air, Dad finds me and gives me a bemused smile. I nearly cry. I see it again—the wreckage, his face, my failure, the depth of his love.

"I figured you might need some help on your first day, son."

"Ah, I was fine," I lie. "Just a little misunderstanding is all."

"Well, you need anything, holler."

Dad and I keep in touch throughout the day with single-sideband radios. They're good for 200 miles in any direction. It helps that Arkansas is flat enough to grind lenses.

Despite my Dad's backing, the following day doesn't go much better. The crew doesn't openly challenge me, but they are still late, arriving in stages and generally don't seem to give a damn. I've been up half the night preparing their flights. My schedule said planes in the air by 5 a.m. Because they're late, it's more like 8 or 9 a.m. Too late and we can't apply chemicals at all. It'll hurt their paychecks but it'll ruin my business.

The third morning, the crew breaks their own record for insolence. Before they reach the hanger, I call them together. They've pushed me past caring. Something bigger than running a business is at stake here. I'm not scared. I'm beyond that. I'm fed up. An eerie calm settles over me.

"Men, listen up. You too, Roscoe. I know it's late. This'll only take a minute. Gonna have a little meeting. Everyone here? Good. Listen, I wanna thank y'all for coming out this morning, and be advised that Nash Flying Services will no longer be needing your services."

I'm expecting their responses.

"What the...?"

"Why, you little bastard."

"Your Daddy know about this?"

"Y'all can't get here on time," I continue. "Y'all are lazy, shiftless, and y'all do just enough to get by. I gotta watch you every second. I got no use for it. Pack it up, boys. I want you off these premises now. *Git.*"

It feels righteous.

They stare for a moment, then with heads tossed high, saunter to their trucks, being sure to slam their doors while muttering oaths loud enough for me to hear.

"Damn little tyrant."

"Napoleon bone-a-part!"

"Princess thinks she's king."

"That boy needs a good thrashing."

And the one I've been dreading:

"Wait 'till I see Bob."

They drive off and I look around. I realize there are still three planes to fly and no one to load them. I can load one, but I'll never get it all done in time.

Dad is waiting for me when I get home late that night. My arms ache. I find him in his usual spot, nestled in the burnt orange recliner with a glass in hand and a bottle of Old Taylor bourbon on the end table. A hurricane lamp casts faint light on a lace doily.

"How'd it go today... son?"

"I fired 'em, Dad."

"So I heard," he says.

"They're worthless, Dad. Can't get there on time. Argue about every damn thing. What good are they?"

"So... how'd you get your fields dusted?"

"I got one loaded myself. I called the other farmers and promised to get out there by Friday. Cut the price a little. They were alright with it."

"You know that's not gonna work, son. Not for long. We ain't the only ones in this business, you know."

"I can't stand it, Dad. I'm there at midnight. I'm checking everything nine ways to Sunday. They show up at six and act like big dogs on a hunt. Who the hell do they think they are?"

"Well...I know who *you* are, son. You're the owner. It's your job to be there at midnight. They're the hired help. At the end of the day, they walk away with a wage but you own the business. They get paid either way, but you..."

"...I know, Dad. I live and die by the business."

"So, what you gonna do, son?"

"Dunno, Dad. Hire more loaders, I guess."

"By Friday?"

"You think I screwed up, Dad?"

"Son, sometimes a warm body is better than no body at all."

"Yeah...I guess you're right."

I pull out my truck keys.

"Where you going?"

"I reckon I got some fences to mend."

I drive to the Smallwood place. It's a singlewide trailer surrounded by dogs on chains, children's toys and rusting appliances. A TV blares from inside. I hesitate, then knock on the thin metal door. Roscoe whips it open and glares down at me. Before he has time to get his mouth in gear, I stick out my hand.

"Roscoe. I'm sorry. I'd like you to come back to work."

He smirks.

"I'll be damned if I ever work for another Nash outfit again, 'specially if you be the one running it."

"I'm paying you $125 a week. How about I give you $20 raise?"

He chuckles.

"Make it $40," he says, leering in triumph.

"I'll give you $30. Be there tomorrow morning, four sharp. Not a minute later."

I turn to go.

"Hey, what about Elroy?" yells Roscoe to my back. "He hired too?"

"Tell him same terms," I say, still walking away. "And no more trouble."

I hear the door slam. A voice booms from inside.

"Ellen, this is Roscoe. Where's Elroy? Get him, will ya? Hey brother, you ain't gonna believe who just came crawling on his knees..."

I go around that night and manage to rehire each and every man at a higher wage. The next morning, I have a couple stragglers — with legitimate excuses — but mostly new attitudes. It looks like Nash Flying Services is getting off the ground just fine.

Dad looks in on me every couple of days. I know he's proud. That's all I need.

Sometimes a poor worker is better than planes on the ground. And humble pie makes a good breakfast from time to time, even for Napoleon.

MAKE ME CRY

1969

"Men don't cry, son."

"No, Dad, they don't. But they sure do bleed."

THE LION'S DEN WAS A DILAPIDATED ice cream and burger joint in Clarendon, Arkansas, named for the local high school team: The Lions. It wasn't the ideal choice for a teenage gathering spot, but it would do until we looked old enough to fool the bartenders across town.

The low-slung building was covered in dirty particleboard frayed at the edges. Halfway up the back, someone had started hanging aluminum siding but gave up and threw on whitewash instead. In front, under the large portico, two windows were designated IN and OUT, and for the reading-impaired, arrows showing the same. The windows were draped in cobwebs full of twitching moths, flies and spiders. A yellow fluorescent light crackled on and off above each window. Off to the side hung a blue-white bulb surrounded by metal grating electrified with enough juice to fry anything seeking enlightenment from the glowing presence within. The odor of their crackling immolation mingled with the burgers and fries and cheap cologne; the scents of innocence driven mad by desperation.

The remote location meant we could laugh and drink and fight as long as nobody broke anything, although what constituted damage to this shack was anybody's guess.

On autumn evenings when the heat of the day broke and humidity fell like tears on a jar of tea, we staked our territorial claims and formed our battleplans. We were tribes of misfits in an oil-soaked parking lot of pickup trucks and beater cars, not quite men but no longer boys.

We played the game, of course. Faced with an adult, it was *Yes sir* and *No ma'am*. But among ourselves, it was a testosterone-fueled war. We came armed for battle. Insults and boasts led to shoves and fists. Reputations were won or lost by a single swing, a lucky strike or a well-placed retort. The prize—bragging rights and the adoration of females.

Me, I had my own reasons for being there. I needed to breath, to observe and to fight.

I was a loner. I didn't join alliances. I wasn't tall or strong compared to boys who spent all summer hoisting hay bales into barns. My strength came from family—Dad and uncles, our businesses, customers and a confidence beyond my years. Which is saying a lot in a community where six-year-olds drove tractors and rose before dawn to milk cows while city kids enrolled in self-esteem therapy.

I settled for being quick on my feet, fast with my fists and smart. I was the watcher, the introvert, the sleeper, always calculating. Who's the wimp? Who's the big dog? Who's vulnerable? Who's a threat?

This approach made me a success in business and kept me alive in the competitive arena of male adolescence. I didn't go to the Lion's Den to test my physical prowess. No... I went to vent my rage.

Years before, as I recovered from the encephalitis that nearly killed me, my parents' divorce finished what the disease had started. Dad was determined to make his boy the toughest man-fighter on the planet. Mom was terrified to let me out of her sight. Swings and slides and bicycles were off-limits while I was in recovery. Funny how I was always in recovery.

Yet sissies and momma's boys were easy prey in the schoolyard, especially boys small for their age. I learned quickly that the shortest distance between two points of view was a fist to the jaw. Arguments had a way of ending once the blood flowed. Better to be the one throwing the punch, but that wasn't guaranteed. I had a lot to learn about fighting. Fortunately, I got a lot of practice.

As I grew up, I came to realize that not everybody thought we Nashes were the preeminent family of the Southern United States. Strange as this sounds, some folks actually despised us. I couldn't understand why. Dad was the greatest man alive. He and my Uncle Roland were the strongest businessmen in the area. And everybody knew who held influence over the sheriffs and judges in our neck of the state. *Why would people hate us?*

Yet the Nashes were the ones everybody wanted to beat. And that was all right with me. Dad and Mom tore me apart. Hate couldn't heal me, but it held me together.

Rage fueled me. And cold logic led me.

That night at the Lion's Den, groups from competing high schools were arriving in packs. As words were being tossed around, I stayed in the shadows with a couple associates. We were nearly done drinking anyway, looking for something else to do.

I had shared a bottle of bourbon and always carried a half-full pint in my pocket, impressing those around me with my ability to buy booze at sixteen years old. It was easy, really. Dad had a standing account at the liquor store and sent me every week to pick up his allotment. The store was fine selling to me as long as I used the drive thru. Whenever I said, "Dad wants an extra bottle added to the order," it was never questioned.

Normally, I didn't drink when I went out — the half-pint was for show. I wanted to look like I'd been drinking. I had an identical half-pint at the house. Let fools think I was drunk. They'd swoop in for the easy kill and I'd beat the crap out of them.

But tonight was different. I was well-nigh lit and feeling just fine. As the different camps came rolling in, I smelled blood in the air. The night was pregnant with possibilities.

Surveying the parking lot, I heard the strains of a Merle Haggard song I liked coming from a custom Ford pickup. Only two boys in our area could afford a truck like that, and my money was in farm equipment stock.

Pierce Williams and his gaggle of friends slithered from the cab and scanned the crowd. I hated each and every one of them. They made a show of finishing their beers and tossing the cans on the ground. I knew Pierce well. He was an older boy from another town — tall, blonde, naturally well-built and he knew it. He wore a custom shirt, belt buckle and handmade boots that I was sure had never come near a plowed field. Everything he had came from Mommy and Daddy's checkbook. He hadn't worked a day in his life.

He didn't like me much either. I couldn't blame him. As one of richest families in the area, the Williams resented the Nashes as much as the Nashes ignored the Williams.

Pierce sauntered to the window and gave his order to the rapt junior high school girl as if he was gonna let her have his baby. I was circling in for the kill.

Bide your time, Clay. Let chumps boast and bullies smash. You'll get your chance. Wait for your opening.

Life was theater to me. I liked guessing what would come next. It was how I earned my fortune by seventeen, taking it from fools like Pierce. It was also why I could only be myself when I was alone. Tonight was different, though. I'd let down my guard. I was drunk in public and cutting up with some friends. The greater the crowd, the greater the clown and... the pain.

Rage was flowing from my wounds. It was time to cut someone else in on my bounty.

As if on cue, the rival schools took up taunts.

"Hey, you see them baby lions last week?" hollered Pierce to his entourage. "I thought they knew how to play football!"

"Yeah, against the cheerleaders," said one of his minions.

"Nah, they don't know the first thing about what to do with a cheerleader," said Pierce.

The crowd laughed, all but the Clarendon boys. This was their home turf.

"Yeah, you say that. We play you week after next, Pierce. We'll see who's talking then," said one of their biggest boys.

But Pierce was just warming up.

"I saw them lion cubs last week sitting on the sidelines crying!" he said.

"Get out!" hollered a minion.

"Nah, it's true," Pierce said. "Whimpering like babies."

"Hell yeah, I saw 'em too," said another. "They were losing so bad, they were holding hands and crying. Awww... Their mommas was trying to console them. It broke my heart!"

"So sweet," sang a boy.

"The hell you say!" came the Clarendon reply.

But everybody knew it was so. Last week's football game had gotten out of hand and the Lions were seen bawling on the sidelines.

"The hell with you, Baxter," shouted a Clarendon boy.

"Aw. I'm sorry. If I lived in that shack your family calls a home, I'd cry too."

"Oh yeah? Well I heard your daddy's a crying drunk. They found him facedown weeping in some whore's lap."

"Yeah, he was begging your momma to let him go home."

The alchemy was intoxicating. I couldn't take much more. From my oblique angle in the dark cover of the arena, I threw back my head and hollered into the crowd words that I would regret for many years to come.

"I'll tell you one damn thing. NO MAN CAN MAKE *ME* CRY!"

Shocked silence.

"Clay Nash. That you back there?" called out Pierce.

Everybody knew the Nashes weren't bullies. We never started fights, we finished them. But tonight was different.

As if drawn by a mating call, Pierce Williams walked up with his friends and poked me in the chest. It was supposed to hurt. I smiled. He was a head taller; that just made picking my targets easier.

"Oh yeah, Nash? Is that so?"

One look at his soft hand and I laughed. This wouldn't take long.

"Nice finger you got there, Williams. Where'd you get your nails done?

"You Nashes think you're all that," he said.

"I'm sorry, Williams. Your people are just too stupid for us to bother with."

"I'm gonna bother you, Nash."

"Nice shirt, too. You buy it yourself? Oh, no. What am I thinking? Mommy took you shopping, didn't she? You're not gonna like what happens to it, Williams. You better start making up your story, 'cause you ain't gonna wanna tell her that I thrashed your ass."

Watching him muster a comeback only confirmed my suspicions. The *fight* wasn't in him but the *bullying* was.

"No man can make you cry, Nash? Wanna see about that?"

Puff went the finger again.

His friends were getting excited.

"Make him cry, Pierce. Make the baby cry!"

Pierce forced up a laugh. "Your daddy's a drunk, Nash. Chasing skirts all over town. And your Momma's a..."

My finger to his chest cut him off. Good thing, too. I'd have killed him if he'd finished that sentence.

"No man can make me cry, Williams." I said. "Not even a boy like you."

As I'd hoped, the fear in his eyes gave way to fury.

Get ready, Clay. He's right-handed.

He took a swing at the side of my head. I blocked it easily and countered with the cross I'd been saving all night. I felt his jaw snap. His eyes pinched closed. He raised his hands as he staggered backwards. Two blows to his unprotected gut quickly followed. He doubled over.

I began using light jabs to his face to lead him around the parking lot, enjoying his acute realization that his ass was mine.

"Who's crying now, Williams? Eh? Come on, boy. Sucker punch me again. My momma's a what, Pierce? Come on, boy. Say it like a man. Here, take this home to your momma. Tell her the baby needs a new shirt."

My fist met his nose and the blood flowed.

I was having a good time...*too* good a time. The alcohol was rushing to my brain and all I could do was laugh. Gasping for breath and panting, Pierce hollered for his friends. From far away, I heard echoes of something my uncle William, the infamous bar fighter, once told me: *No matter how good the plan, the enemy always gets a vote. Never turn your back on an enemy, Clay.*

I realized my mistake a second too late. One of Pierce's friends jumped me from behind while another grabbed my feet. I had let myself be surrounded. Six of them hauled me down and began kicking me with the steel-tipped boots we all wore in those days. My miscalculation hurt, but their blows were like nothing I had ever felt before.

I'm losing... badly.

I lashed out, trying to get to neutral ground, but Pierce urged them on. Protection was useless. My body instinctively curled into a fetal position. I tucked my elbows into my gut and buried my bloodied face against my shirt. I tasted steel and blood and felt torn lips against broken teeth. I convulsed as my kidneys took shot after shot. My mind exploded with colors as their blows landed on my swollen eyes and temples. I was defenseless, beyond pain. Utter blackness ended it all.

I woke up a week later in the hospital, and for the second time in my life, I amazed doctors and nurses who didn't expect me to live.

What happened at the Lion's Den that night was unheard of in our day. While fighting was a part of our culture, killing was not. We all carried weapons. We all drove pickup trucks, mostly for hauling deer, wood or machines... or to pass out drunk. Knives and firearms were common. Everyone hunted, everyone lived near the woods. What city folks called survival was normal to us. The difference was, where we could split each other's lips, blacken eyes and even knock out teeth with fists, we never took to anything more. Weapons were for working and hunting. Hands were for fighting.

At the end of a fight, more times than not, we helped up the guy we had just beaten, broke out our bottle and gave him the first gulp of whiskey, laughing as it stung before making everything better. Fighting was bonding, a test of manhood, the path to brotherhood. We weren't killers. That's what made the beating I received that night so much worse. It didn't simply break my bones; it broke the code. You could mess a man up; you couldn't try to kill him. Not if you expected to live afterward.

In the hospital, shivering between linen sheets, the images flashed in rapid succession: the blows, the voices, the curses and laughter, but mostly the faces. *The faces.* And with each face, *a name.*

Three weeks later, someone came to see me. I cracked open one eye and made out a dull shape. I didn't know it was my best friend, Frank, until he spoke.

"How are you, Clay?"

"They never made me cry, Frank" I whispered.

"They never made you cry, Clay," he said. "And they never will."

Six weeks into my hospital stay, with double vision and leaning heavily on Dad's arm, I told the doctors I was going home to finish healing or die. Either way, I was gone.

"Who were they, son?"

"I'll take care of it, Dad."

"That's not what I asked, son."

Dad never stopped asking and I never told him. I couldn't. He'd kill them. And then their daddies would kill him or me. There were laws against murder, even in the South and the Nash influence could only do so much. I might never see Dad again, and I couldn't live with that.

Besides, I had a plan.

I would heal. I would get stronger. And I would go hunting.

Who were they, son?

I'll take care of it, Dad.

The day I walked up on my first attacker, he was plowing a field. I'd chosen him because he was the least culpable. Wayne was a likeable boy, easily led, a lifelong follower. I drove slowly across his freshly plowed rows. He must have seen my pickup from a distance because he shut off the tractor, climbed down and waited.

I slipped from the cab without a word, my eyes dead on him, omens of death blowing across the fresh earth. He smelled of diesel, dirt and fear.

"I knew you'd be coming, Clay. I heard you got out of the hospital. I'm glad you're OK. Look, I'm sorry. I'm *so* sorry. I didn't mean to hurt you. It was Pierce. You know? He made me. Please…"

He wasn't lying. He hadn't hurt me much, he just hadn't helped. That had to be addressed.

He started shaking as I wrapped my hand around his throat with just enough pressure to squelch his pleas.

"Wayne, they got a town just west of here. You know what they call it?"

He forced his head *No*.

"They call it *Nash Corner*, Wayne. Know why they call it that?"

He whimpered and shook.

"Because we're everywhere, Wayne. And do you know what they call the cemetery there?"

His sweat ran down my arm.

"*Nash cemetery*. Why, Wayne? Why do we have a cemetery named after us?"

Spit foamed from his lips.

"Because that's where we bury our enemies, Wayne.

"Now Wayne, if you EVER cross me again…don't ever cross me… EVER! You got that? I swear to God, it'll be your funeral sure as he made little green apples. And we'll take your damn family with you."

"This is your Get-Out-Of-Jail card, Wayne. Don't waste it."

His garbled gasp and sunken head told me it was done. I shoved him backwards into the tractor and walked away as he stood shaking. He'd have stood there all day if I had told him to.

Who were they, son?

One down, five to go, Dad.

I took my time in the following months, dealing with them one at a time, letting rumors spread, always finding them alone. I broke bones, I busted teeth, I spilled blood. Most of them cried, some crawled away, and some...I can't tell you. No one died. A few might have begged for it, though.

When I found Pierce Williams, he was sitting alone in his truck at the edge of the woods, watching deer feed in a harvested bean field. It was near sundown, a scarlet gash across the horizon, a sure sign of fall. It'd been a year since our encounter.

I'd hidden my truck a hundred feet away and had been observing him for a while. He was probably thinking about hunting season. Most hunters select their trophy bucks early. They watch them, learn their movements and know where to find them when the season opens. Patience is everything in hunting.

Conscious of the fading light, I crept to Pierce's driver's side door, careful to stay in his blind spot. His head hit the cab when I smashed the door with a thirty-eight inch Louisville Slugger. Wet with fear and quaking, it was easy to jerk him from the cab and hurl him to the ground. He whimpered like a baby. Scrambling on the ground, his eyes were fixed on mine, his legs shaking too badly to stand.

"How's it feel to be paralyzed, Pierce? Feels good, don't it? All your friends are running around while you... you're stuck in a hospital bed. Doctors are sticking you with needles, your parents are locked outside, hearing you scream, you wonder if you'll ever walk again. All the while, the son of a jackass who put you there is out getting drunk, getting laid — though I doubt it — and having a big time. You know what that's like, Pierce?"

He eyed the bat and raised a protective arm.

"Clay, no! Please, I'm sorry. Don't hurt…"

The bat made a vicious arc, snapping the proffered limb. Pierce screamed and folded, cradling the limp arm while trying to crawl away. My backswing found his exposed rib cage. Each successive blow brought blood stains and shallower breathing. When he passed out, I started his truck, wedged a rock against the gas pedal and sent it crashing into a tree. With Pierce's body carefully arranged, it looked like an accident.

And maybe it was. Maybe he just got in the way of my war against the world that left me a paralyzed orphan while scum like him lived in luxury.

That's where I left it. That's where I left my thirst for vengeance. I heard later that he refused to say who had done it. Smart of him. No one would ever know for all these years…except the two people to whom it mattered most.

"You hear about the Williams boy? That was you, wasn't it, son?"

"You think so, Dad?"

"Nah, son. I know so."

"Dad, when does it stop hurting?

"Dad…?"

ANNIE

1961 / 1972

IT WAS A SCORCHING JULY AFTERNOON as Annie, Greg and I sat on the steps of the mercantile store sharing an RC Cola under the shade of a blue and white awning. We were the reigning third-graders in this small town and arguing as usual. It was the only way to pass the time before we were old enough to drive to someplace more interesting, although exactly where that was, nobody knew.

Today was about naming the cars that rolled down Main Street. Something about humid weather brought out my competitive spirit. Even if I was wrong, I had to be right. There were no trophies for participation and second place was the first guy to lose.

"That's a '42 Hudson," said Greg with conviction. Sweat ran down his cheeks, forming at the edge of his haircut and staining the collar of his plaid shirt, a hand-me-down from his older brothers. Why he didn't go shirtless like the rest of us boys, I couldn't say for sure. He always was proper, a stickler for rules. That's how he was raised.

"Are you blind?" I said. "Didn't you see the Indian on the hood? It's a Pontiac. I should know. My uncle drove one."

I tipped the RC cola to my lips to punctuate my point. I knew he was right; it was a Hudson. But where's the fun in that?

I glanced at Annie sitting between us. She made a "Arrgghhh" noise and covered her ears with her hands. Her simple sundress hung from narrow shoulders and ended in a frayed hem at her knees. The shorts she wore beneath it enabled her to keep up with the boys. I liked her being around, though I was too young to know why. Hers was a presence as light as a butterfly, strong as a cornstalk, an unbridled spirit beneath a freckled face that often scowled but never scorned. Together, the three of us enjoyed the blessings of childhood in the peace afforded by our un-woke bodies.

"I don't care if your whole family drives a Pontiac," shot back Greg. "I don't care if there are fifty Pontiac Indians on your reservation and half of them are on the warpath. I know a Hudson when I see one."

"Nah, Greg. You just don't like being told you're wrong, "I said, chuckling. "You come by it honestly, though. I'll give you that. All you Site's are pure as fresh-picked cotton. And just as soft."

Now, to anyone else, those would have been fighting words. But Greg's people were fundamental Christians, and he worked hard at being good. Beating him was a breeze. He never cheated, lied or stole. He made it too easy. He was winding up, though, and I waited with a smile. Getting cussed out by the likes of him was a treat. He never swore, he just made up stuff from the Bible to throw at me.

"It was a Hudson, Clay Nash, just as sure as I'm going to heaven and you're going straight to...."

"Stop it you two!" hollered Annie. "That's not nice, Greg. And if you don't shut up, Clay Nash, I'm going to...."

"You're gonna what, Annie?"

"I'm sorry," said Greg, head hanging. "Don't fight. It's my fault. You're right, Clay. It's a Pontiac."

The power she had over him amazed me.

We both knew she'd never finish her threat to me, but Greg was another story. Samson had a better chance against Delilah than my ruddy friend had against this girl.

"Besides," continued Annie, smiling. "It was a Lincoln. Anybody could see that."

We laughed.

"Yeah, it *was* a Lincoln," said Greg, a sudden convert to the church of Annie Lewis.

So, it surprised no one when, at age eighteen, Greg made two fateful decisions that shaped his life forever. He joined the Army and he made Annie Lewis his wife.

When Greg went off to Army basic training, the whole community gave him a heartfelt sendoff. And it was natural for Annie and I to see each other occasionally and share letters from Greg while he was gone. Sometimes I helped with things around the house and we'd have a beer afterwards. I knew I'd never join the service—a man couldn't get rich serving Uncle Sam—but I could help those who served and made my capitalist enterprises possible.

Greg's two brothers had promised to help out while he was gone, but they were worthless drunks. And sometimes, drunks talk crap.

Early one Sunday morning, about twelve weeks after Greg left for bootcamp, I got a knock at my door. It was Greg, fit and squared away in his Army-green private's uniform, a single ribbon on his chest.

"Hey, Greg!" I hollered. "You're back early. How's..."

His hand rose and the muzzle of a thirty-two caliber, nickel-plated pistol hovered inches from my face.

"Well, hey, brother," I said. "Funny way to say 'hello'."

"Shut up," he barked. "Get inside."

"Easy now, Greg. What's going on?" I said, raising my hands and backing up slowly. "The Army get to you? Nice gun, by the way. Whoa now, take it easy. That thing loaded? What's going on, Greg?"

"You tell *me* what's going on," he said.

Something had him on a hair trigger. I chose my words carefully.

"Greg, relax. Something's got you riled up. Have a seat. Let's talk about it...whatever it is. It's sure not worth all this."

"Sit down," he said, motioning me to a chair at the kitchen table. He took the one on the other side.

Forcing calmness, I took in my familiar surroundings, possibly for the last time. The lacquered wood trim along the ceiling, the avocado green Formica table, the fluorescent ceiling light, the plates from breakfast still in the sink, water dripping from the faucet. I made a mental note to install a new washer.

My captor glared at me, his hand shaking.

"Greg, things are getting a little crazy here, don'cha think? Maybe we can put down the gun. I've got whiskey in the cupboard I've been saving for you. Wanna drink? Whatever it is, we can work this out. No reason to get excited here."

"WHERE'S ANNIE?" he screamed.

"I don't know where Annie is, Greg," I said. "You ask your bothers? I'm guessing she's at home. It's early yet. You been to the house yet? Is she missing?"

"How long you been sleeping with her, you no good piece of crap? Was it going on before I left?"

"Whoa! Hold on, brother. Is that what you think? You think I'm the one who's been... Who's been talking to you, Greg? Bill and Earle? 'Cause there ain't nothing that..."

"They seen you. Don't lie. You're not going to get out of this one, Clay."

"Greg, there's nothing to lie about. Sure, Annie and I meet up sometimes. We share stories. We might have a beer at the house. Hey, the other day, I tacked up that siding that was coming off your barn. That's it, Greg. I'm telling you, that's it! If something's going on, it ain't me."

"NO MORE LIES! I'm gonna kill you, Clay."

"You're not gonna kill me, Greg."

"I learned a thing or two in the Army, Clay. You're not the only tough guy around here. I'm gonna kill you and then I'm gonna kill myself."

"Now Greg, why you wanna do that?"

"I can't live without her, Clay. I love her too much. I can't...I just can't take it anymore."

A tear rolled down his cheek.

"I know, Greg. I hear you, man. I know how much she means to you. And she loves you, too. Listen, this whole thing is a big misunderstanding. Somebody's gotten into your head and filled it with lies. It's doing you a world of harm. Doesn't the Bible say 'Ye shall know the truth, and...um, the truth is always right'? Doesn't it say that? This ain't right, Greg. Nothing about this is right. You can't come barging in here putting a gun to my head. Is that what Jesus says to do? Hell no. Now, why don't you set that thing down and let's have that drink. I'll help you find whoever's bothering Annie."

I slowly reached for the gun but he jerked back... a little too quick for my liking.

"Get away from me, Clay. I mean it this time. I'm done with all your foolin'. It's over this time. You're gonna die for what you done. I'm gonna kill you."

"You're not gonna kill me, Greg."

"How do you know?"

"Because if you were gonna kill me, I'd be dead already."

The realization dawned on him like sunrise over a junkyard. I had him.

"You're no killer, Greg. You never were. The Army taught you to shoot. It didn't teach you to kill. Yeah, you could shoot me, but it'd be for a lie, and you'd have to live with that for the rest of your life. You ready for that, Greg? Ready to live with that on your conscience? And what would Annie say? She'd say 'You big, dumb jerk! I loved you.' But she'd be saying it across prison bars, Greg. Now don't be stupid. Hell, if it's me, you can always kill me later. But if it ain't — and it ain't — you can't bring me back to life. Come on now. For me, for you... for Annie... put that thing down and let's talk."

That's when he broke into sobs, the gun shaking with every heave. At this distance, his aim would be wild but anything could happen. I slid a box of tissues his way. He wiped his face with his sleeve.

"I reckon I'm not much of a husband," he cried. "I don't know who to believe anymore. Who's telling the truth? Who's lying? What's going, Clay? What's happening? She stopped writing. I could tell something was wrong. Bill and Earle told me they saw you coming to the house at all hours of the night and you weren't the only one. And I'm stuck in camp and going crazy and the Drill Sargent's screaming, 'Don't worry, son. When you get home, you'll find her just as you left her—pretty as a picture, waving and smiling and freshly kissed.'"

"Come on now, Greg. You don't believe that."

"I DON'T KNOW WHO TO BELIEVE!" he screamed.

His head dropped as he slammed the gun on the table. I waited for an explosion that never came. He covered his face with both hands and I slid the gun out of reach.

"Listen, Greg. Whatever you've done or haven't done, it ain't worth killing for, is it? She loves you, brother. Go home and make things right. I'll be there for you. We've always been friends. We always will. We'll get through this together."

His sobs slowed.

"I don't know...I don't know...I don't know anything anymore."

With that, he stood up, turned and left through the same door he'd come through to kill me.

I sat at the table for a long time imagining his face, his voice, my kitchen walls splattered with blood. I was shaking now, my forehead clammy, my strength reduced to a bounced check on a bankrupt account.

Closing my eyes, I forced my mind clear, walked back to the bedroom door and opened it.

"He's gone."

Annie came out in her pajamas, tears flooding her young face. She looked up at me.

"Time to go home, Darlin'," I said.

She nodded nervously, scurried about gathering up her things, and slipped out the back door without a word. I would never see her like that again, nor could I. I was a long way from giving up my philandering ways, but I knew one thing. I was through cheating with friends' wives.

Greg and Annie mended their marriage, and after the Army, he became the best carpenter in the area. His work can be found in state capitals and private offices of corporate presidents. Greg and I renewed our friendship later in life, and if he ever suspected the truth, he never let on. I was grateful. I contracted him to install a gun cabinet I'd ordered in Memphis, one with space for forty weapons. As an avid hunter and collector, I use them all from time to time. But there is one locked away in a drawer that I can never bring myself to touch again—a thirty-two caliber nickel-plated revolver.

NIKKI

<u>1972</u>

IT WAS LATE, FAR PAST MIDNIGHT. I was tearing down an old logging road, slicing through the Arkansas humidity of deep summer. I checked my watch, grabbed another gear and flogged the screaming engine. Heavy night air bathed my face through the side vent. It was gonna be close. The truck bounced over rocks and limbs as I fought to keep it between the ditches. Trees rushed past, their low branches whispering a warning: *Love and lust, daggers and friends!*

Any sane man would have turned around, but it was too late for warnings... and I was anything but sane.

Flushed with liquid courage, the boy riding shotgun was in high spirits. Jeff was my best friend, the son of a good Christian family. He was soft in the center and easy-going. Folks teased him for his flaming red hair and freckles, and bullies loved to push him around, which is probably why he stuck close to me through high school even though we were a grade apart. What he lacked in aggression, though, he made up for with a quick tongue that caused as much trouble as it saved. He could talk himself off the cross, but how'd he get there in the first place? Still, it'd served him well a time or two, especially with one Nikki Olsen.

Nikki was the finest girl in town, tall and blonde with eyes that flooded a man's soul with blue light. Her little sister was a carbon copy in miniature. They were the daughters of old man Olsen, a tough Norwegian who came to Arkansas for the rich bottom land of the river valley. Turns out, he wasn't much of a farmer, but he grew fine young women. He taught them to work like field hands. Many a day, Jeff and I would drive by the Olsen place just to watch those girls on their Massey Ferguson tractors. We'd park for hours as they drove back and forth in the hot sun. It didn't hurt that they wore bikinis. No, that didn't hurt at all.

I gripped the wheel and doubled down on my resolve.

Jeff wasn't much of a drinker, but tonight he was lit up like a Christmas tree waiting for Santa. I couldn't wait for him to pass out. Anything to shut him up. Instead, he stuck his baby face out the window and screamed into the wind:

"I'm getting married tomorrow. Oh yeah. Married. Hey, Clay, did you hear? I'm gettin' married. Whoo hoo!"

"I'm the best man, Jeff. Or maybe you didn't notice."

Red hair danced as he sang.

"She's the most beautiful girl in the world. And we're gettin' married! Hey Clay, listen to this:

"I think that I shall never see
A bride as lovely as a tree.
A bride whose rich, sweet flowing breasts
Make a place to lay my head.

"Hah ha ha. I made that up, Clay. It rhymes, you know? Whatya think?"

"I think you should use your mouth for something useful."

I shoved the bourbon into his hands and counted the seconds to his house. Letting up on the gas, I peered through the dirty windshield for the road out of these woods. *Gotta be here somewhere.* That's when I saw them — a row of pines dead ahead where the road should have been. I'd overshot the turn.

The whisky at tonight's rehearsal dinner had gone down smooth... maybe too smooth. This was gonna be rough. I had seconds to react. Pale headlights showed three curves hard right where only one should have been.

Dad's voice flooded my mind: *When there's more than one, son, always aim for the middle. And if that don't work, close one eye.*

This wasn't a bar fight, but it'd do. Three never worked for me anyway.

One shot, Clay. Make it perfect.

Jeff, oblivious to it all, tipped the bottle to terminal depth.

"Hold on!" I yelled.

His scream told me he saw it too.

Strange what the mind does when faced with the finality of its existence. As my friend searched frantically for a seatbelt that didn't exist, I offered some advice.

"Security's just a myth, Jeff." I hollered.

In the cold logic of terror, I saw an alternative.

I could end this now. Slam into these trees. They'd find us in the morning and the papers would write about the tragedy of two young men – a groom and his best man – killed the night before the wedding.

But my survival instincts had other ideas.

Downshifting hard and counter steering, I slammed the truck into a slide, throwing a rooster tail of red dirt and gravel into the waiting pines while the front aligned itself with our portal through this dark night. Finding traction, the rear wheels shot us dead-center into the turn. We exploded out of the forest and into a meadow lane of wildflowers bathed in moonlight.

The headlines would have to wait.

With the road before us suddenly calm, I grabbed the bottle. It was meant to be. All of this – Jeff, Nikki, me, the road; it was our destiny. As Jeff curled in terror against the door, I let the liquor burn a new path into my soul.

We were getting near his place. I wiped the sweat off my watch. Minutes to go. Jeff was whimpering. I had to calm him down.

"You remember your vows, Jeff?" I said.

"That was some crazy stuff back there, Clay!" he cried.

"Nah," I hollered. "I just wanted to show you some fun before you sign your life away."

"I'm in big trouble then," Jeff said. "I think you scared the words right outta me."

"Ah, just make 'em up. That should be no problem for you."

He laughed.

I knew his vows better than he did. Every detail of the rehearsal that night flashed before me. Jeff standing uneasy, staring at his boots. The preacher taking us through the ritual. The piano chiming to life. A tall girl in a plain dress gliding up the aisle on the arm of her Norwegian father. Fresh flowers in her hair. Her shy eyes. Jeff's shudder as she took her place. Angels whispering. Piano falling silent.

Suddenly I'm beside her, reaching for her hands, waiting for the vows. The preacher is scowling and reads from his book: *"Love and lust, daggers and friends!"*

"Shut up!" I yelled into the truck.

An unbuckled Jeff leaned over, grabbed his head and burst into tears.

"I can't help it, Clay. I love her. I swear to God, I love her so bad. It scares me sometimes, you know? What am I gonna do? She's so far above me. I don't know how I ever got her. She's a gift, you know? She's God's gift to me. How'm I gonna keep her, Clay? How'm I gonna keep a woman like that? I don't know a thing about women. Not like you, Clay. God, you've had hundreds... thousands."

"I tried to fix you up a time or two, Jeff."

"You know I get all tied up when it comes to women. But Nikki's different. She's the one. You know? I'm scared, Clay. I feel like she's the one and I'm scared to death. I never knew what love felt like. Not like this. It hurts, Clay. God it hurts. Is it supposed to hurt? I can't stand the thought of losing her. How'd I ever live without her? You know what I mean, Clay? Know what I mean?"

"Yeah, Jeff. I do."

As his house came into view, I steered for the floodlight in the middle, the second time that night I had to choose one from three. The smell of hot brakes filled the cab as I slid the truck to a stop inches from the door.

"Get some shuteye, boy. You got a big day tomorrow," I said, shoving him toward the door.

"I can't move, Clay. My legs aren't there."

I staggered around the truck and peeled back the passenger door. Jeff spilled from the cab like a newborn calf. With his arm over my shoulders, I dragged him inside and dropped him into bed. Jeff sunk into the mattress. A rented tux stared at us from the far wall. Before Jeff passed out, I had to hear one more confession. I owed him that much.

"You're mah best friend, Clay man," he slurred. "Clay Nash, best friend of... Do you, Robert Clayburn Nash, take this woman to be Jeff's lawfully... awfully... waffley... wifely... Zzzzz...."

A gold band shone on the nightstand. I turned it over in my fingers, reliving the day he'd bought it. *FOREVER* was inscribed on the inside. It had been my idea.

Forever's a long time, Son, Mom had said. *Especially toward the end. Whatever you decide, do it all the way. No regrets.*

"No regrets, Mom."

Regret was never a problem for me. I could make a bet, lose everything and keep on rolling. Dad taught me that. Ever the entrepreneur, he once bought a hay baler, rented his services out to farmers, and was doing pretty well for a week until a rock got stuck in the gears and the belt caught fire. The thing burned to ashes in minutes.

When he told me about it later, he was smiling.

"Dad, you just lost five thousand dollars."

"Ah, heck, Son, I was gettin' tired of bailing hay anyway."

I gazed at Jeff, an innocent babe surrounded by perfect angels.

"It was meant to be, brother."

I left the light burning.

Back in my truck, I counted the minutes to home, grab the things I'd thrown together, and get to the Olsen farm. I drove like a fiend, the radio screaming every song Hank Williams ever wrote.

I finally slowed when I reached the rugged driveway. Headlights off, I saw a faint light in the kitchen. Nikki loved candles.

New bride nerves.

It was the same kitchen where the three of us had planned the wedding. Not a grand affair. Jeff didn't have much money and Nikki even less. The honeymoon was gonna be a one-night-stand in a motel.

You want more, don't you Nikki? You deserve it.

I tapped at the door, its glass panes rattling in cracked glaze. My hands gripped the gifts. I waited and tapped louder. The door was loose in its frame. Old man Olsen wasn't much of a carpenter either.

God, let him be a sound sleeper.

A shadow appeared. I drew a breath as the door shuddered open and Nikki Olsen stood before me, her summer robe backlit by candlelight, a Norwegian goddess fallen to earth. In that moment, I knew what I wanted in life. No more, no less.

She smiled.

"Clay, what are you doing here? What's all this?"

"Here," I said abruptly. "And...and this. Here."

I shoved a bouquet of flowers and a white teddy bear into her arms.

She stared at the bear, then back at me with merriment.

"Clay Nash, what's this all about?" she asked slowly.

She didn't have to ask.

Make sure she knows before you tell her, Mom said. *I know you get tongue-tied, son, but women don't need words. They just need your heart.*

"Nikki... let's... get... Oh hell, Nikki. You don't have to marry Jeff tomorrow. You can have me. I'm the one you really want. I see it in your eyes. I've got money in the bank. I've got more coming in. I'll take you anywhere you want to go. Atlanta, New Mexico, California, Canada. Yeah, I'll even take you to Canada... if it's summer. You know I can get you there, girl."

"Clay...?"

"And we'll settle down. Build us a house. I can find work easy. We could make a good life. I'm mechanical, you know? I can fix anything. Folks say so. Anything. Anything at all. You could get work waiting tables, and when the kids come along, I'll be making enough for you to stay home. I swear I'll buy you anything you want. Anything."

She was gathering her thoughts, but this was no time for thinking.

"Nikki, get your things and let's go. We'll figure it out on the way."

She took a long time to answer.

"Clay, it's not like I'm not flattered, OK? So don't take this wrong. But there's no way in hell I'm going anywhere with you. I'm not gonna hurt that dear, sweet boy for all the gold in Fort Knox."

"I know, Nikki. I don't want to hurt him either. That's why we gotta leave right now. Get it over and done with. Memphis airport is only two hours away. We'll be long gone by morning. Nobody'll know. Jeff'll be fine. I know him. We're best friends! I'll write him a letter and explain everything. Nikki, I know what you want. Jeff can take you to the next county. That's not a honeymoon. That's not a life. I can... I can... Oh hell, Nikki... I can take you to the stars."

She laughed, and that was the death of me.

"Clay, I'm sure there's a dozen other girls that would take you up on this. God knows you've got plenty. Why don't you..."

"No, Nikki! They ain't nothin' to me. You're the one I want. I can't stop thinking about you. Ever since I saw you and Jeff together, I knew we were meant to be. I just couldn't say it. I still can't. But that's how I feel. You do too. I can see it in your eyes. You know this is right. You feel it like I do. Let's not waste our chance. It's meant to be, Nikki."

"Clay, *thank you*. It's not every day that a girl gets two suitors in one night. I get that you think you're in love with me — or whatever you wanna call it — but I'm spoken for, alright? And that's just the way it is. Now, you take your sad-eyed teddy bear and go home. Give them flowers to your momma and sleep off whatever's gotten into you. I'll see you at the wedding. You and I are friends, OK? Let's keep it that way. And we'll never talk of this again. Now go!"

And with that, the door closed on Nikki Olsen.

I stumbled back to the truck expecting her to come running after me calling my name, saying *sorry* and that it was just too sudden and give her a minute to pack.

She didn't.

It should have worked. I should have had her. She should have been on my arm, squeezing in close, laughing and crying as we rode off and left all this behind. She should have been making excited plans for where to go first, her eyes flashing as she sang the names of the places we'd explore together.

She wasn't.

I didn't get it. I had everything: money, opportunity, guns, a teddy bear. It should have worked.

It didn't.

Yet somewhere from faraway, a light was dawning. Maybe...just maybe...driving a tractor in a bikini didn't mean what I thought it meant. Maybe she saw something in Jeff that she didn't see in me. She was different. I didn't know if I loved her, but I wanted her, and I should have been able to take her. Jeff was a good kid, but he was nothing compared to me. It should have been me standing beside her. It should have been easy.

It wasn't.

The charges against me were mounting. Someday, there'd be enough to rescue me. Repentance comes easy under the weight of overwhelming guilt, especially when you have nothing left but ashes.

I once heard that the definition of insanity is doing the same thing over and over again and expecting different results. Soon, I'd be given another chance to make things right. And I'd aim for the one in the middle.

DAWN OF DAY

1974

IT WAS THE WEE HOURS OF A SUNDAY MORNING, not yet dawn, when I pulled the ski boat into the landing on the White River. I shook Jennine and Lois, the women who had been with us all day. Their sunburns drew sharp lines where their bathing suits had been.

"Wake up, girls."

I handed my truck keys to my buddy, Frank. My speech was thick with beer.

"Frank, I'm gonna pass out."

"You and me both, Clay."

"Take me home...leave boat on the trailer...I'll get 'er in the morning."

"It's morning, Clay."

"Oh hell, you know what I mean."

Our passengers groaned and fished for their tops. I was way past any female entanglement.

Let me go home to die.

"Come on, girls...party's over...everybody bed...go now," I mumbled.

At the sound of *bed*, Jennine giggled and ran her hand across my chest. But I was having none of it. I could barely stand.

"We gonna ski tomorrow, Clay?" she cooed.

"Call later, sweetheart...go on now...go home"

As the girls stumbled to their car, Frank got the boat secured. I slipped into the passenger's seat of his truck and embraced the darkness. It was rare for me to be so drunk that I couldn't drive, but the day had been a hot one and the beer was cold, oh so cold.

"Watch out...will ya?" I muttered, jarred awake when Frank ran into the shoulder. "You sure you're OK? I can drive if...if'n...if..."

My eyes drifted back into the void.

Seconds later, bloody screams ripped me awake. The first thing I saw was Susan's flowerbed. We were in the middle of it.

"Frank Daniels! You ever tear up my flowers again, I'll blow your ass to kingdom come. You hear me?"

Awake now, I looked out the driver's side window to my sweet bride, all of eighty-eight pounds, holding a 357-caliber pistol at my buddy's head. Even in the starlight, I could see the fear on his face. I knew Susan could shoot; I never dreamed she could kill. Apparently, the same realization was hitting Frank.

"I'm sorry, ma'am. I guess I just missed the driveway."

"Yeah, well let me tell you: I don't miss a thing. I'll put your brains all over this cab."

And then in kinder, gentler tones reserved for the Lord and Master of the house:

"Clay Nash! Get out now or join him in hell!"

I cracked the door, leaned into it, and rolled into Susan's freshly planted gardenias. The fragrance of crushed pedals and rich loam blended with the beer-puke soaking my shirt. Susan came around to my side with a garden hose and began spraying me off. I curled in a ball, howling at the injustice of the cold shower. I heard Frank's truck tear off into history. I thought of all the nights he'd driven me home, never stopping, just slowing down and shoving me out the door. He picked the wrong night to stop.

"Take me with you," I moaned to the flowers.

Icy water in my face brought me back to reality.

"Now get up!" said my blushing bride.

Susan jerked me by the collar, led me into the garage, ordered me to strip, then shoved me onto the old couch in the family room where, mercifully, I passed out again, only to be unceremoniously awaked by a divine light intent on separating the lobes of my brain. The smell of bacon told me this must be morning. I just wasn't sure which morning.

It was a day or two later before I worked up the nerve to go out again, but Susan and I had an unusual relationship in those days. *Easier to get forgiveness than permission.* Dad, Uncle Roland and I ran several businesses together, and life was good, if you went by the money. I traveled frequently, met a lot of people, and mixed business with pleasure in ways that she was mostly ignorant of.

Susan had her faults, but her greatest was that of innocence. It was that trait that I took full advantage of until the day I could go no further, when I collapsed with the full weight of my sins upon God's mercy and Susan's forgiveness. This was not that day, however.

As Susan tended our newborn, Dawn, I made the usual excuses and sweet-talked my way out of the house and down to the river—saying I had to retrieve the boat. Instead, Frank and I and the girls had fun skiing and drinking and exploring small islands. We caught some bass and Frank seasoned the fillets to perfection as we reveled in the high time of an afternoon we'd stolen.

Mindful to stay a bit soberer this time and needing gas for another ski run, I was coming back to the landing about midafternoon when I saw a thin figure standing on the shore and holding a bundle. I got closer and my heart skipped. It was way too early for my usual moment of reckoning. The party had just started. This was a hangover without the drunk.

As the boat glided to the pier, I sensed what was coming and lowered my head to receive it.

"Clay Nash, you have a choice," Susan said evenly when I was within earshot.

Everyone in the boat stiffened. Lois and Jennine reached for towels. Frank took the controls. I walked to the bow. Susan continued, her head high.

"You either come home with me now, or you'll have no home to come to!"

Her voice was even, steady, resolute. It'd have been better if she was hysterical. In that moment, I saw why I'd married her. She had a strength I did not possess.

"I mean it, Clay. I'm not taking it any more. This ain't no life. This ain't no marriage. You want pretty little tramps? You wanna live like a single man? You go right ahead. But without me. Oh, and you can say goodbye to Dawn. Say goodbye to Daddy, baby. And be glad you never had to grow up knowing him. Make up your mind, Clay. Playtime's over. This is for real."

My mind was made up the instant I saw her on the shore. I turned to Frank, gave him the keys, told him the boat was his, and waded ashore to my wife and daughter.

We went home that day and we were a family... for a while. I still had a long way to go. *The sins of the father...* But it was a beginning.

NIKKI REVISITED

<u>1975</u>

THREE YEARS WENT BY, Susan and I were married, and one day I heard that Jeff and Nikki had hit a rough patch. He'd been caught cheating. I guess my influence finally surfaced. She was filing for divorce—I confirmed this through mutual friends. Here was my chance to make things right.

Finding her number, I called her one night but hung up when she answered. I tried three more times. On the fourth, I found my voice.

"Nikki, it's Clay. It's a damn shame what Jeff did to you."

"Clay, I never want to see that cheating son of a bitch again!"

"You never will, Nikki. Not if I know my once-best friend. He wasn't worthy of you."

"It's good to hear somebody say that, Clay. His family all says it's my fault. I wasn't a good enough wife. I didn't love him right. We didn't go on vacations. We never went anywhere. Can you believe it? I'm sick of all this mess."

Hang up... now, Nash!

"Nikki, the truth is, you've probably been lonely for a long time. I understand that. I'm lonely too. I want you to know, girl, that if I had a woman like you, she'd be on my cherish list and I'd never take my eyes off her."

"Well, that's kind of you to say, Clay, but...."

She's right, you fool!

"Nikki, I'm not talking about anything we shouldn't do. I'm just saying that you deserve some attention and I'd love to give it to you. You know I'm married. Everybody knows that. What they don't know is that Clay Nash is about more than hopping into the sack with any woman he finds. You taught me that. I care about you, Nikki. And I just want us to be able to help each other."

"I don't know, Clay. Think how it would look if...."

"Who cares, Nikki? Listen, let's get us a place for a couple hours, just for privacy, and we can relax. I'll bring a few things. You still like that white wine we had at your wedding? I'll have some cheese and crackers and we can watch TV, listen to the radio, anything you like. And in the end, I'm headed home. I promise. I just want us to talk. Nothing more. Could that work for you?"

"I appreciate your friendship, Clay. I do. There're just some things I'm not ready to...."

This can't go any further. Give it up, Clay.

"Nikki, I understand you're hurting."

"I HATE THE SON OF A BITCH!" she screamed.

"I don't blame you, Nikki. It hurts now, but it'll feel better soon. A lot better. I promise."

"God, I hope so. Maybe some time out would do me some good. White wine, you say?" she chuckled.

"Chilled on ice, Nikki."

"Alright, Clay. Let's do this. Heck, he deserves it. And we'll talk about the old days before all this crap started."

"So, tomorrow night? Holiday Inn, route 90, just outside of Barkley? Say, seven o'clock?"

"I'll be there. Thanks again, Clay. You're a special person."

I hung up the phone and wanted to throw up. The nagging voice was growing louder every time I cheated. Still, I was running on auto-pilot, playing a role I knew by instinct.

I turned the yellow pages to florists and ordered up a batch of flowers. The rest of the day, between my other responsibilities, I gathered the wine, the cheeses, breads and crackers she craved, even plastic plates—everything for a motel picnic. For dessert, a bottle of George Dickel's smooth Tennessee whiskey. And just for good measure, I found a white teddy bear.

I left for work the next morning with a crumbling wall between me and my conscience. Susan kissed me goodbye like she always did, wishing me a good day and smiling, but this morning it held a sincerity I had not noticed in a while, a sweet innocence that took me back to when I fell in love with her that day on an elementary school playground.

She was eight; I was nearly eight. An older woman — I should have known. She was doing the broad jump in gym class and I was hanging out at recess trying to look nonchalant. She wore jeans, cowboy boots and a plaid shirt. She was tan from summer vacation. I was instantly smitten. We became best friends and hung out together all through school. We'd eat lunch together almost every day. We rode bikes, motorcycles, went fishing. We even went frog gigging. That's when I knew it was real.

But she would never date me. I think it was the heathen in me. It took me years to wear her down. I asked her to marry me so many times, I lost count. Sadly, much of my courage in those days came out of a bottle. Then one day she came home for a weekend during her second year of college and I knew. I just knew. It was in the way she hugged me. It was going to happen this time.

Our dating was rocky, but she never caught on that her fiancée was a womanizer. I was smooth and Susan was ignorant of the darker side of life. She was so pure that she simply could not imagine anyone being that two-faced. I loved her. I still do. I was just following a bad script in which I was the star.

The morning of our wedding, Dad sat me down with some sage advice.

"Son, every man's gotta have a good woman and a mistress."

"Dad...?"

"Hush, boy. I know what you been doing. Now listen. From what I can tell, you're getting a good woman there."

"Yeah, I am, Dad. Lucky man. Like when you married Mom."

"Listen, son. A man's gotta keep his good woman and his mistress apart. About forty miles does it. Too far and your good woman wonders where you're going all the time. Too close and she catches on. Forty miles is about right, son."

As he rose to go, I did a quick calculation. She was about ten miles away. I made plans to move her as soon as possible.

All this ran through my mind that morning as I hugged Susan and told her about a business meeting that evening with an important customer. If we got this contract, it would be big money for us and I'd take her somewhere nice. She seemed excited and she kissed me again in that childlike way as if nothing else in the world mattered but her man and the love we shared.

I barely made it out the door with my lies intact. Whatever was left of my self-respect had just been decimated by her trust. I drove to work that morning, went around back to the dumpster and chucked it all—the wine, cheese, crackers, even the teddy bear. A two-time loser, that bear. Must have been tough on him. Some bears never learn.

I never went to the Holiday Inn that night, and I never called Nikki to explain what happened. I figured my absence would say it all. The shame of leading her on and then standing her up tore at me, but so did the thought of violating the love of a little girl in cowboy boots who once jumped 3 feet, 7 inches just to impress me.

HOME

I know you're married. So am I. See? Nah, my wife doesn't drink. I just come here for the music. Thing is, I been watching you from back in the corner. Yeah, that was me in the shadows. And I just want to ask you one question, if you don't mind. What's a pretty woman like you doing out here alone at this hour? Oh? He did what? The man's a fool, you know that? I'm just gonna say it. A fool like him doesn't deserve you. I'm Clay, by the way. Yeah...one of them damn Nashes. That's right. We're not so bad when you get to know us. And you're...Alice. Yeah. I've seen you in here a time or two. But this is the first time you've been alone. Takes some courage for a lovely lady to come in here alone. What are you drinking? Hank, two whiskey sours, please. So yeah, I know George. Yeah, that had to have hurt. I don't understand men like that. Everything they could possibly want in the whole wide world is right in front of them and they think they gotta run off and chase something strange. Doesn't make sense. Alice, I wanna tell you something. Just to help you. If I had a woman with your pretty smile, I'd spend the rest of my life making sure that smile stayed on her face. You know that? Hey, you don't have to cry. Here, your makeup's running. There, that's better. My God, you're a pretty little thing. Well, listen, I just came by to make sure you were alright. You probably want to be alone at a time like this. It's never easy when you find out the truth. I can... Oh, a smoke? Sure. Why don't we go out back to the parking lot. Get some fresh air. You know...Hey, I know a place we could go. Get some peace and quiet. Just you and me? Yeah? Come on, finish your drink and let's go.

It was that easy. Married women were the best, rich married women even better. They didn't want to get involved. They had a man. They had money. All they were looking for was exactly what I could give them—a one-night stand. You don't look for the *lay*; you look for the *leave*.

I also had my regulars. Because I traveled all over the region, it was convenient to set something up in whatever town I found myself, always with the promise that I'd be back for some quality time when my schedule allowed.

Yeah, I'll be in town on Wednesday. You wanna meet? Yeah? Remember the old graveyard out on route 40? The one with that big oak tree in the center and the little white chapel. About two o'clock? Yeah, I still have the green GMC. See you then. Hey, bring a blanket, will you?

It wasn't all predatory advances, however. Just as the Nashes were not bullies, neither were we outright abusers. Sure, I took advantage of lonely women; I regret that. But sitting in a bar, seeing a man plying a gullible woman with alcohol just to get her in the cab of his truck was too much for me. As with fighting, we had a code for seduction. Women were fair game as long as they were game. Rape was not a game. More than once, I followed a man out to his truck, heard the familiar muffled screams and tearing of cloth, and ripped him from the cab with a vengeance he'd not soon forget. The shaking woman holding her shredded blouse while I bloodied her attacker had nothing to fear from me, just a safe ride home and some sage advice.

"Honey, if you're looking to get picked up, this is the place. If you're looking for friendship, this ain't the place. Try the local Sunday School. Darling, the men in here play for keeps. Ain't one of them I'd trust with my dog. Nobody's friends after the third drink. You think they're paying out all that money because they like conversation? It's a meat market, darling. You don't want to be meat, don't come here. Now, get inside, lock your door, and if he shows up, you call the sheriff. He knows me. Just tell him Clay Nash got you out of a jam, and he'll take care of you. Trust me."

You could think of it as a hunter who loved watching deer run through an open field but hated the poachers who took game out of season. I was an honorable philanderer, if there is such a thing. I possessed a deep respect for women even as I took full advantage of their weaknesses. It was mutual... or so I thought.

Time has a way of teaching us, and such a conflicted point of view could only stand so long.

One night, about midnight, I was driving home from a hookup. She was the wife of a wealthy builder. She'd caught him cheating with his secretary—I was so thankful for young secretaries in those days—and she was out for a little revenge sex. From my vantage point in the recesses of the Golden Rail Saloon, I read her from a country mile. I applied my charms, and we followed a well-worn path.

As I headed home, I counted my blessings. I just got some action. Hank Williams Jr. was on the radio. I had plenty of bucks in the bank. Dad and I were inseparable. Susan was home with the kids and never suspected anything. And I was known throughout these parts as a shrewd businessman you never crossed twice.

I considered the story I was going to tell Susan.

It got late. The customer wanted to hear this band in the next county. I was too drunk to drive so I took a nap in the cab.

It was the delivery that mattered. Rehearse it until you believe it, then say it with a clear conscience. And always... always... stick to the story.

It is the truth, by God! I swear!

Yet something was gnawing at me. What was it? Did I leave something out of my story? Did I mess up and say something to that woman I shouldn't have? Did I forget to use protection? Was there a farm account I'd neglected to service? Was my accountant stealing from me? Was my truck misfiring? Did Hank miss a note?

I searched and searched for a flaw in this web of happiness and came up with nothing.

Nothing... at all.

Just a growing emptiness.

Before long, I was leaking. I couldn't stem the flow pouring from my breached hull. It was White River there in my truck and I didn't know what was making me cry.

You don't do that, Clay. I don't care if you did beat the shit out of a guy last month for wasting a pretty woman. You're not much better yourself. Sure...rules. What rules, Clay? You got a pretty woman at home who loves you. What did you promise her on your wedding day? Were you even there? Did that rich woman you just left sleeping between cold sheets have any feelings for you? Was she even thinking of you at all? You know she wasn't. She was cold as a well digger's ass. She used you just like you used her. For what, Clay? What are you even doing out here? It's 2 a.m. and you're a grown man making up lies to cover your tracks.

What's a man, if not his word? If they can't trust you, they can't depend on you. What good are you? You want to be doing this when you're eighty? Chasing tail and lying about it? You got money in the bank? So what? What's that buy you? A new truck every year and your nights spent sucking down the smoke of a hundred losers while you scrounge the lounge for the scraps left by other men's failed marriages? What are you, other than another damn loser?

I was crying pretty hard by then. I pulled the truck over. I knew where I was. I just couldn't go any farther.

It's over, Clay. It's done. That pistol in the glove box? You might as well use it. What's a slow death compared to a quick one? That's your whole life, ain't it, Clay? A quick one? Nobody gets hurt if nobody cares? Well...who's hurting now, Clay? Who cares more than you?

I finally made it home that night and slipped through the backdoor from the garage. I knew from her breathing that Susan was asleep, so I'd only need my story in the morning. Time to perfect it. Before I lay down beside her, however, I crept into Dawn's bedroom and spied on her sweet, round head, her breath mingling with mine, the tranquility of a full belly, warm covers and colorful dreams.

I made a promise that night to my daughters, my son, my wife, myself and whatever God I imagined was out there. I was done. The cheating, lying, using, predator was done. I still held no stock for religion, the Bible, church or a host of hypocritical conventions masquerading as repentance. Tonight, under the banner of the Nash family domicile, I honored its inhabitants by taking one step closer to being the man I was created to be.

My children would find fear elsewhere. They would learn to lie and distrust far from these walls. Here would be their safe place. I would give my life to ensure that.

I was home.

TRUCKIN'

I got ten forward gears,
And a Georgia overdrive.
I'm taking little white pills,
And my eyes are open wide.
I just passed a 'Jimmy' and a 'White'
I've been passin' everything in sight.
Six days on the road
And I'm gonna make it home tonight.

Dave Dudley

ART MILLER WAS DRUNK. That, by itself, was nothing to cause folks in Little Rock to exclaim "Oh my!" In fact, few people cared except for a precocious twelve-year-old biding his time in the passenger seat of his Uncle Nash's tractor-trailer.

It never failed. Art would get his daily route from my Uncle Freeland Nash—a four-hour run from Wheatly to the grain mill in Yazoo City. He'd show up showered and clean shaven, but Uncle Freeland was hard to fool. Today was no different.

"Art, you sober today?" asked Freeland. "No, wait. Let me rephrase that. 'Hey Art, *how* sober are you today?'"

"What? I'm sober every day," Art replied. "What do you think I am? Some good-for-nothing drunk? You gotta lot of damn nerve, Freeland. Have I ever wrecked on you? Missed a delivery? Gotten in trouble with the law? By God, I got a good mind to quit right here and now! You can find another driver to haul your junk down the road."

Of course, Art knew every lawman in these parts. They were his drinking buddies.

I'd give anything to drive truck. Then one day, watching the usual exchange, I saw my chance.

"Uncle Freeland, I can go with him. I'll read the map and keep him company. I'll help unload the truck."

"Good idea, Clay," said Freeland with a glance at Art. "Keep an eye on this ol' cuss. If he gets in any trouble, I wanna know about it. You got that, son?"

"Yassir. I'll keep an eye on him. Sure will, Uncle Freeland."

"Ain't gonna be no trouble, Freeland," said Art, clearly insulted. "And I don't need no whelp tagging along just to snitch on me. I reckon he can keep me company, though. The radio in that truck's busted again. You know any Waylon songs, boy?"

"Nah sir. I can't sing. But I can read a map. And I can fix anything that ain't..."

"A map? Boy, I know this route blindfolded," said Art indignantly.

"Good thing, too," said Uncle Freeland. "'Cause he drives with his eyes closed!"

I clamored into the cab and did a quick check. Wires hung under the dash. Half the gages were cracked or water-filled. The cab smelled of oil and exhaust. The seats were covered in cracked leather.

It was heaven.

Art climbed in the driver's side, tossed a glance at me and began the process—half mechanical, half superstition—to get the old motor coughing and spitting to life. I watched his every motion, memorizing the steps, absorbing his curses like prayers.

He ground first gear into place, popped the clutch and rocked the truck forward, following up with the next gear a tad too late by my reckoning. I started to ask a question about when to shift but he barked.

"I ain't hearing no Waylon, son. You best get that radio going or warm up them pipes."

I fiddled with the wires under the radio, found a short and a blown fuse, and had it blaring out pure country comfort before we saw the first cop.

"Hey-ah, Amos!" hollered Art as we drove by.

If Officer Amos detected anything unusual about my chauffeur, his casual wave didn't show it. Aside from keeping the aging semi between the white lines, we rolled down Route 49 like they'd paved it just for us. It was when we came to the small town of Marianna, just south of Wheatley, that things got interesting. Art pulled over in front of the All-States Liquor store.

"Be right back, boy. You want anything? Good job on that radio, by the way. They said you could fix anything. I'm beginning to believe 'em."

Minutes later, I was munching a moon pie and an RC Cola as Art broke the seal on a pint of Old Granddad and ground the gears to get us crawling out of town again.

I watched the road, playing it back in my mind.

We made it to the mill in Yazoo. The foreman must have been related to the cop. "Hey Art. Back 'er right up here. M'on back. M'on back. <CRUNCH!> That's good." I helped unload our trailer and when we were empty, I climbed back in the cab to find Art slumped over the wheel singing with the radio.

> *I've been...um...Mississippi,*
> *Uh...New 'Leans,*
> *Yeah...*
> *Played in California,*
> *Nope... much hain't seen.*
> *No there ain't.*
> *Well, I'm ramblin' m...man,*
> *Don't fool...I'm...uh...ramblin' man.*

I felt my pulse quicken. Dad had taught me to hunt deer, to track them without being seen, to anticipate the unexpected. I saw where this was leading — exactly where I'd hoped it'd go.

"Come Art, you gotta drive," I said unconvincingly.

Art didn't move, he didn't stir, only sang louder, and this got the attention of the mill workers who just chuckled and shook their heads. Apparently, they'd seen this show before.

I grabbed Art with all my might and got him moved over to my side. Then I went around to the driver's seat. There was a case of oil behind it. Uncle Feeland's trucks ran alright, but they didn't run far without a constant supply of Texas tea. The case got me high enough to see over the dash and yet still reach the pedals. I was on my tip-toes but I knew what to do from all the times Uncle Freeland let me drive around the yard. Without a second glance at the amused workers, I found first gear, shaved off an inch or two of metal, let the clutch out kinda rough, cut the wheel and doubled clutched straight into third gear.

We were rolling. I couldn't have been happier

I guess some folks might have seen this situation for what it was—an outrageous assault fostered by a raging alcoholic on the safety of an unlicensed minor intent on getting his Uncle's truck back to its rightful home.

From my perspective, I was having the time of my life.

As we rolled down the state road, I tried hard to look older. The case of oil helped. Art came to every now and then to mess with the radio station or to tell me: "You're do fine, Jeff. Trained ya right, I done. Now keep yer eyes on the... on the...."

I made sure his bottle stayed within reach.

I guess I wasn't so innocent after all.

It was sad to see Wheatley. Of course, I never told a soul what happened. Next week, I was back in the cab with Art. We made a good team, him drinking and me biding my time 'till I got the wheel.

Trucking would be in my blood forever. My life's calling had been found. Which was perfectly understandable. From the time I could hold a rattle, I was a mechanical prodigy, a wonder with all things motor and machine. I took things apart and reassembled them, usually for the better. At six years old, I had a job repairing magneto generators with Mr. Dupree at the farm equipment business. I made enough to buy better tools and expand my repertoire of services offered.

With Art serving as my trucking mentor — I learned all of Waylon's songs — it wouldn't be long before I was driving all through high school. I had a nightly run to Helena and was always back by 3 a.m. to grab a couple hours sleep before classes started. Living in a farming community meant the teachers understood my comings and goings and occasional naps between classes. My photographic memory came in handy. I could pass any test. That didn't mean I learned anything, but I acquired enough to get by. Besides, they weren't there to train the next generation of rocket scientists. We were all gonna be farmers or work in related industries. I was just ahead of my time.

Over the next few years, Uncle Freeland migrated away from the trucking business, selling off his trucks one by one. And I was there to buy them. By age sixteen, I had my CDL license (now that I could drive legally) and a '57 GMC with chicken-catcher doors. I could make my own runs hauling cotton seed and grain from surrounding farms to the mills.

The farm equipment business that Dad and Uncle Roland ran also brought me a lot of work. In time, my fleet grew to five trucks, and I hired drivers to free me up to start a mechanical equipment shop. I was the chief mechanic, known throughout the area as the best in the business. My trucks regularly broke one-hundred mph, law enforcement permitting (or sleeping), of course. And I was driving truck as well.

Life was good. Trucking was regulated, which meant we had regular runs at set prices for our labor. Our shop included welding and fabrication services. We could turn sheet metal into bumpers with nothing but a ballpeen hammer.

I was flying high. The local bank held an open loan for me that I used to buy and sell all kinds of things. My skills for business, mechanics, bargaining and people finally came together. I was printing money and spending it just as fast.

Married by now, my homelife was another story, mainly because I wasn't there. It wasn't just work. It was bars and women and customers and friends. It all flowed together like a well-stirred cauldron. The anger that carried me through my teenage years wasn't any better, however. I drank a lot of whiskey and I fought a lot of men. The pressures of earning a living and caring for my family only made things worse.

It was about that time that Susan's parents started praying for me. Courageous people, my in-laws. They had been going to a Methodist church, got saved, and now were reaching out to their family. I knew I needed God. I just didn't know God.

I was working over a hundred hours a week in those days, living on prescription speed I got from a Cuban doctor who supplied the local farmers so they could get their crops harvested.

Our most lucrative runs were hauling rice to the Gulf of Mexico for shipment to Russia, a country long on boastfulness but short on the ability to feed itself.

Life was so good that I was beginning to think nothing could mess it up.

Enter President Jimmy Carter, a son of the South and, at that time, the destroyer of my world. Now, don't get me wrong. Jimmy was (and is, as of this writing) a good man, a *principled* man. But sometimes principles and trucking don't mix. When Jimmy decided in 1979 to end grain sales to Russia to retaliate for their invasion of Afghanistan, it might have bothered the Russian people a little (until other countries stepped in to take our place) but it devastated U.S. farmers and nearly destroyed my trucking business.

I say "nearly" because it took another decision by President Carter to finish us off for good. In 1980, for better or worse, he deregulated the trucking industry. Suddenly, the price supports we'd banked on to buy trucks, equipment and hire drivers were gone. What wasn't gone was the crushing debt we'd assumed in the process.

Still, I can't fault Jimmy. He did what he thought was right, and maybe it was. Ironically, his decisions changed my life... for the better, although it took me years to appreciate that.

To this day, I can imagine him yelling at his advisors in the Oval Office, hammering a fist on the wooden desk that had served presidents for two centuries.

"What have we done to get Clay Nash saved?"

"Well, Sir, we shut down rice shipments to the Gulf."

"Yeah, well apparently that wasn't enough. I hear he's still working and drinking and carrying on — things I can't imagine, being the good Baptist man that I am. We need something to get him under conviction. Bring him to his knees. Teach him what a Christian man is all about."

"Sir, we have a plan. We'll deregulate the trucking industry."

"Outstanding! Do it."

And so, they did.

I was three quarters of a million dollars in debt, selling off trucks at sacrificial prices, losing my best drivers and fighting to hold onto my most profitable routes. Everyone was cutting their rates and the bottom was nowhere in sight.

Facing bankruptcy, Susan and I made a fateful decision. We would pay back all that we owed and dig out of this mess somehow. I would start driving as well as running the trucking business and mechanic shop. It meant living on five hours a week and more speed, hallucinating regularly and teetering on the edge of breakdown. But we'd pay it all back somehow... assuming I survived.

The bread and butter run for me was from Memphis to L.A. I carried rice to the Uncle Ben's plant in California and returned with produce for the local markets. Leaving on Saturday afternoon, I could make the run to Cali in thirty-four hours. Owing to my mechanic skills, I regularly ran my diesel at 110 mph through the Texas night. This was strategically planned. The State Troopers didn't have a nightshift working the deserted interstate.

Amphetamines could only get me so far, however. Often around Weatherford, Texas, just west of Dallas, I'd pull over at a truck stop and, with tears in my eyes, climb into a phone booth on the far side of the parking lot.

Hi, Honey, the kids in bed? Aw, good. Hey, listen, I'm thinking about turning around. No, really. Now... Wait... Listen to me, will ya? I don't think I can take this anymore. Not this time, not tonight. Maybe next week. It's a bad night. Real bad. I should have slept before I left, but I had that truck to get out of the shop. Yeah, I took my pills. I'm awake; I just can't see straight. The lines are all over the road. I got gravel coming up on me. It's not good, I tell ya. There was a truck appeared outta nowhere, came straight for me and disappeared at the last second. I got a bad feeling about this one. Like...I'm not gonna make it. Something bad's gonna happen, I just know it. I got that itchy feeling all over my skin like bugs are crawling on me. My hands won't stop shaking. They're coming for me. I feel them. They hear me, you know? They're listening in to this call. They know what I'm thinking. I hear them breathing. They're getting closer... closer.

Yeah... I know what we owe. They can have it. Take it all, the bastards. What else can they take? They won't get much from a dead man. Take my truck, you bloodsuckers. See if you can do any better with it.

Don't you hear me? I'm telling you, I'm not gonna make it. I can't. I can't....

Ok... Ok.... Let me see if I can at least get out of Texas. If I make it to El Paso, I know I'll be right. Yeah, you're right. It's just that I'm seeing things that ain't there, you know what I mean? I hate that stuff. It scares the hell outta me. So damn scared. I can fight men. I can't fight phantoms.

Alright... yeah... I'll call you from L.A. No... don't worry. I just needed to talk. OK? Yeah, I'll see you soon.

I'll get some rest when I get home.

I promise.

I love you too.

BY GRACE

Through many dangers, toils and snares
We have already come.
T'was grace that brought us safe thus far
And grace will lead us home.

1981-1982

AS I SAID, SUSAN'S PARENTS had found God's salvation in a small Methodist church. Susan and I started talking about going to church there because of their encouragement. Truth be told, it was as much to get them to leave me alone six days a week that I attended their church on the seventh.

Susan had a different take on things — not the first time for our marriage. She had experienced the new birth a few months earlier. I noticed the difference in her, but I didn't know what to call it. She was at peace, more so than when it was just me caring for her.

I didn't begrudge her this newfound life. Whatever she had found, she deserved it. I wasn't the greatest husband, although I certainly wasn't the worst. By my standards, I worked like a dog and never left her or the kids bereft of anything that we could possibly afford. My love was in my work. My passion was in my absence. I drove myself harder than I drove those trucks. It met two needs. I earned a living and I stayed gone. The road was my home, my antagonist, my provider, my mistress. It gave me what I needed and sometimes what I wanted. Yet it never left me satisfied for long, only appeased for another week. I was in a death spiral, that corkscrew descent that an airplane slips into when the pilot has zero visibility and doesn't know he's slowly going down... until he crashes.

My standards were falling. It was fog all around me but the sensation of motion kept me distracted. Any motion was good. It meant I was alive. Or so it seemed.

*****

Lib McClain was the mother of my best friend, Frank, the same friend who'd come to see me in the hospital after my near-death experience at The Lion's Den. I'd grown up around her; she was a second mother to me. A righteous woman, kind and gentle, she could see straight through me, yet always with eyes of love. She was one of the few Christians I admired. Most of my world was populated with hard-working, hard-loving heathens. It pained her to see me grow to be just like them; I could read it in her eyes.

I respected her as much for how she loved me as for the life she endured. She'd married young, had children, and then her husband was drafted into World War II. He was assigned as a flame thrower in an infantry unit. His job was to incinerate enemy soldiers. The memories of their screams as they fled was too much for him to carry home. He returned and spent the rest of his life rooted in an easy chair, slowly drinking himself to death, as Lib tried in vain to bring him back to life.

The love in that woman would have been remarkable for any life. For one that had seen so much suffering, it was miraculous. Her passing grieved me as deeply as any blood relative's.

Years later, as a grown man still finding his way, I sat up one night reading an article in Reader's Digest. It was about a father who took his two young daughters and older son on a wilderness adventure and ended up marooned. It struck me how closely my life matched his. I also had two daughters and a son. This father had to make a terrible decision. He knew that only he and the son had a chance to make it out alive. The daughters could not—they were too young and he couldn't take them. So he did the only thing possible. He left them behind, took the son, and went for help, knowing that his return was doubtful. It was their only hope. Fortunately, he succeeded.

Engrossed as I was in that father's life-or-death dilemma, something happened that helped drive me into God's arms of salvation. As I sat alone that night contemplating the story, I heard the voice of Lib McClain speak as clear as anyone in the room.

"Clay, you're a good man, but you need God."

It shook me to my core.

One evening found me at Susan's church where one of the members, Grace Thompson, was teaching from the

Bible. She was giving life to the scriptures in a way I'd never heard before. I sat in the back row, alone with my thoughts, surveying the crowd—my usual mode of operation. Susan was visiting her dad in Louisville. No one really knew me in this church, yet I knew everyone. I was the watcher, the schemer, the weigher of hearts and minds. Tonight was different, however. I could feel it. I was being watched. The hunter was being hunted. Not by anyone I could see, though. The eyes on me were coming from another dimension.

Conviction bore down upon me. I couldn't get much lower. I was strung out from a year on the road, constant drug infestation, nightmares and nervous breakdowns. My hands shook. I couldn't go into most bars anymore; I was too well known. People were either looking to settle an old score or looking for a handout. I was easy prey. I'd given up infidelity—the guilt had finally gotten to me—but there was nothing to take its place. I loved Susan—always have—but how to love her, how to be married, was a work in progress. I loved my kids, too, but most days when I did make it home, I was passed out in bed. I lived far from their busy lives of school and friends and growing up. I was a stranger among those who should have had the best of my heart. Instead, I was filling a role I'd seen Dad live, and it was killing me and all I loved. I finally had to admit that I needed something beyond what Dad could ever give me. I saw the outline of the answer but I couldn't fill in the missing pieces. It was a calling beyond anything I'd ever known.

For months, there had been a growing pressure on my chest. It was like the Titanic had settled on me a thousand leagues under the sea. It was squeezing the life out of me. The time had come to pay the full price for my choices or go down for the last count. It'd been running a tab for so long that I couldn't count the debt. I wasn't even sure what passed for currency anymore. My life was worthless. My businesses were broken. I was a stranger in my own home. Nothing from nothing spelled _Clay Nash._

It was at that point, sitting in that back pew, scanning the congregation for posers, imposters, weaklings and hypocrites, I came to the devastating realization that there was nothing left to lose. Why not give my life to God? There was no way but up. Soon, a simple prayer escaped my lips.

"Jesus, they say you can change me. And if you can, you'd better do it. I can't stand the man I am any longer."

I felt to walk to the front of the church. Grace had finished her teaching and was wrapping up. I stood in the pew and all eyes turned to this disheveled stranger in a tattered hunting shirt, greasy jeans, full beard and dark hair wild as wind. My hands shook worse. I knew my eyes were bloodshot. They always were in those days. Halting steps carried me forward, my legs long accustomed to hours of tension cramped in the cab of my Freightliner semi. Every step was lighter but also harder. I was on new ground, unstable as I was. The weight was slowly coming off my chest and I realized how much I needed it to feel grounded. This felt like flying... or floating, at least. The roaring in my ears — another permeant fixture — was clearing, and I thought it unusual that no one was speaking. It was suddenly a church of Quakers, yet I was the only one quaking.

Finding the railing at the front was a welcomed relief. Ignoring the alarm in Grace's demeanor — it sure didn't seem like they got many like me saved in that church — I knelt before God, the universe and all creation, for the first time in my life. My prayers bled from my heart. He heard them before I spoke them, and I knew... I just knew... that I was welcomed in his heart.

I'd met my match. I thought of all the men I'd fought to prove myself, all the women I'd seduced to amuse myself, the trucking business I'd built to justify myself. I remembered Billy, the drifter I'd tried to kill that night along the White River and come away convicted, empty, shattered. In all that I'd ever won and lost, nothing had ever answered the cry of my heart like God.

God, are you there? was answered by Jesus on a cross, the one who rose from an empty tomb and sits at the right hand of the Father God.

Dad was a good man, but he was just a man. I needed a father who could save me. I needed my creator, my savior.

He answered me with love. That evening, all my strength gone, leaning against the Methodist rail, Jesus poured into me the balm of forgiveness. There was no excuse for what I had done, nor for what I'd become. There was only love transforming me into what I would someday become.

Eternity embraced me as I wept at that altar, loving every second — the soul-wrenching confessions, the mercy poured into my wounds, the love engrafting me into God's heart, and the assurances that all I loved was in his mighty hands. It was no longer up to me alone. I had given it all I had. No man ever tried harder to be the god he needed. If my life meant anything at this point, it testified that no one can go it alone. Sure, we can do some things well without acknowledging God — people do it all the time — but driven as I was to advance myself and live my life to the fullest, I experienced the utter and complete futility of all my efforts. I surrendered completely, as much as I knew how, and it was overwhelming.

I finally stood, oblivious of time. The room had been washed clean. Colors that seemed dull and unfocused before I knelt now burst forth in brilliance, matching the rebirth I felt within. The eyes of the congregation were still on me, but they had changed as well. I would soon learn that while I had learned much from the back pew, it would be to the front that I was called. All that came later, of course. At that moment, surveying the Body of Christ as a new member, I had just one question: *Why do they all seem scared of me?*

So deep, so personal was my conversion experience that I could share none of it. Instead, I nodded to a bewildered Grace and made my way outside and into the night air rife with the promise of new life. A man standing near me had a halo. Looking up at the moon, it was redolent with hope, a pure light washing and restoring me.

God, let me stay this way forever.

Finally, I began to think practically. It was time to make amends. Forgiveness is priceless, a gift beyond words, but amends take a bit more work. I wanted to reveal who I was and what God had just done. It started with those I loved the most.

I called Susan's mom to tell her, but she beat me to it.

"Clay, God told me that you would get saved tonight."

Really? She knew? You know, God, you could have saved me all that trouble of going to the altar.

Susan and I made plans to start this new life together. It wouldn't be easy; we both knew the other too well. No blissful fairytale about happy-ever-after was going to work with us. No, this was going to be a tale of after-ever-happy. I knew God had changed me. I also knew there was a lot of changing to do. He showed me that he was ready. Now, I was too.

This life would be... the Real Deal.

TURNAROUND

1985

For now we see through a glass, darkly; but then face to face: now I know in part; but then shall I know even as also I am known.

1 Corinthians 13:12

WELL, THERE YOU HAVE IT. Saved. Forgiven. *The Real Deal.*

Sanctified? No. Perfect? Not hardly. Saintly? Ask me tomorrow. Maybe next week. Better yet, ask Susan. No... wait.

In the three years after my salvation experience, any expectations of a blissful glide to heaven went up in smoke. No, I didn't backslide. I didn't resort to the old ways of deceit and decrepitude. I simply lived life... and life happened.

See, before Christ, a man is traveling down a dark alley heading toward death. He can see it afar off, and the farther he goes down that alley, the worse things look all around him. Rotting trash, rusted cars, shady characters lurking in shadows, black cats screeching, signs saying "I'd Turn Back If I Was You."

You get the picture.

Now, if he heeds the Lord's stirring and accepts Jesus in his heart, he'll stop before reaching total annihilation and turn back to the light that he left long ago when he began sinning. It's an about-face, a 180-degree turnabout. He goes from facing death to facing life.

Only one problem. He hasn't changed position, only direction. The decay is still around him. Trash is still rotting; rusted cars are still rusting; warning signs are still grammatically incorrect. Some of his ways change, but now he has to walk out of what he walked into. The death he was walking towards, he is now walking away from. Yet the harbingers of death are still there, filling his nostrils with stench even as life bids him forth. His old friends still call, his thoughts still wander, entrenched fears still lurk, and the debts and broken relationships he neglected during his hell-bent charge into sin still need to be addressed.

He's a new man—he's aligned with Jesus—but he's got a long way to go.

The godly change at salvation is in the man's orientation. And as long as he stays focused on the light, he continues moving away from darkness and into the eternal life that Jesus promises. He learns truth in place of lies. He learns love in place of hate. He learns Holy Spirit in place of Satan. He acquires an authentic identity through Jesus in place of a false identity though his flesh. And he is aware of Almighty God walking with him.

It is a process.

Yes, God can, and does, miraculously deliver us from dire circumstances. And the release from the power of death—its consuming hold over us—can be so overwhelming that we think God has perfected us right on the spot. We are suddenly new men and women!

Alright! Somebody book my next crusade!

Yes, all things are made new... in time. That's when the reality of God's sanctification catches up to us. All things are *becoming* new. We are all works in progress.

This can be daunting to a newly minted Christian, especially one with so much to forgive. I mean, we all need forgiven. I get that. But I wasn't your average choir boy seeking to rededicate his life at Christian camp after guzzling the communion wine. No, I was being raised from the prone position, flat-out sucking dirt, one foot in the grave and two hands digging furiously. As Cain famously declared: my sins were too great for me to bear. I was broken. I had to be. Not everyone is ground to powder prior to salvation, but I was, and for that...

... I am eternally grateful.

The one who is forgiven most, loves most.

Jesus didn't just save me—although that would have been good enough for any man. He did more. He saved those I loved—my wife, my family and my friends. He saved my life.

I was still driving trucks. I had to. Money was tight and our creditors were getting ninety cents of every dollar we earned. The IRS got the other thirty cents and we lived on the rest. Yeah, even though I dipped a line in the water every now and then, I'd yet to find a coin in the mouth of a fish. Still, God was providing in other ways. I was being taught to believe and receive.

Instead of dropping speed to stay awake on the road, I learned that praying an hour in the spirit was as good as an hour's sleep. And driving somewhere near the speed limit had its blessings as well. Fewer tickets, for one. But also, less stress of always being on edge, striving to stay one step ahead (or behind) the law.

I learned the myriad ways that God speaks to me. To do so, he opened me up to the spiritual world. Of course, there are many things in the spirit that aren't of God. Sensitivity to spirituality is not synonymous with holiness. Not even close. No more than stepping into a boxing ring means you're the middleweight champion of the world. You're more likely to get your head knocked off than be crowned the next Cassius Clay. (Good name, though.)

As I struggled to keep my businesses afloat, I began to have dreams, nightmares really, about dying in a horrific trucking accident. It was disconcerting. I tried to push them aside with my fledgling spiritual strength, but truth was, I didn't know what to believe. Was this God warning me? The devil tormenting me? Or something else altogether?

(Anyone who thinks the things of the spirit always make logical sense can stop reading now. This is a non-fiction book.)

I was confused and terrified. I'd soon find out that I had good reason to be.

HIGHWAY OF GOD

1985

IT WAS THE 31ST OF JANUARY, 1985, a day I'll always remember. We were fighting to survive. Susan was home with the kids and doing everything she could to keep us going. We were down to two trucks and a prayer and leaning heavily on the prayer. Months prior, God had told me to get out of the trucking business. I did not sense an immediacy to the word, however, just an indication that he was moving us in that direction.

That day in January, when things couldn't get any worse, the man I'd assigned to drive one of the trucks, a '79 Freightliner, brought it to the house and quit on the spot. This left me in a terrible bind. I needed to get that truck to Little Rock to be loaded but there was also work in the shop I had to finish for a customer. Adding to the stress, a buyer was coming for my second truck—soon we'd be down to just the Freightliner—and I badly needed the cash from that sale. So, I called my friend, Sean Owens, who was driving for my Uncle Freeland at the time.

I knew Sean well. We were in school together from the eighth grade until our senior year. We didn't graduate together, though. I got kicked out for various and sundry offenses, some of which were actually true. Those who knew me called it a promotion. I reckon it was... for the school.

I explained the desperate situation to Sean. *The driver quitting. The work in the shop. A buyer coming.* I practically begged him to take the truck to Little Rock to get loaded and bring it back to the house. It was a simple run, but it would free me up and further Nash Enterprises for another day.

At least, this is what I told him. And it was the truth... mostly. Just not the whole truth. There are some things you can't share with another person. They'd think you were crazy, and who knows... maybe you are.

The other reason I needed a driver was that I'd been having nightmares. In my dreams, I was driving the Freightliner—it was always that truck—when a load came crashing into the cab and crushed me to death. It was so real: the shattered glass, the screams, the smell of blood, the weight crushing the life out of me. So terrified was I that I refused to even drive the truck across the parking lot.

Ironically, I'd always been partial to that truck. It had been mine from brand new. I wrecked it once, but did not total it. Knowing what the insurance company would do with it, however, I took a sledge hammer and knocked the oil pan off to make it look like the motor had been destroyed in the wreck. The adjuster was convinced and added the cost of a new engine to the settlement.

It took me a year to rebuild the truck. It was a labor of love. God gave me spiritual insight on how to do it, and I rebuilt it exactly as he showed me. When I finished, it was better than new. Despite its ability to run at triple digits, the truck was safe. It passed all the DOD inspections and was ready to roll.

And it did. Until the nightmares.

The only person I shared my terror with was Susan. A man can be vulnerable to his wife. To other men... not so much.

Sean agreed to take the run. I knew he would. He was one of those guys whom everyone loved. He was short, even by my standards, but he was the life of the party, even by my... ah, never mind. He came from a good family. He struggled a bit with drugs and depression — we all did from time to time — but he always had a cheery answer to a bleak circumstance. I loved to be around him. Oddly, he never married. The only immediate family he had was a son born to an ex-girlfriend, a boy he doted on.

Against the backdrop of my nascent spirituality, struggling businesses, abject financial conditions and nightmarish visions, I bid Sean goodbye that morning and went about my other duties. I looked forward to seeing him again in a few hours, having a couple beers and swapping manly stories, hopefully with a few dollars in my pocket from the day's work. Meanwhile, the buyer showed up and bought the second truck, leaving me just the Freightliner that Sean was driving.

I got the call about six hours later.

We don't get much snow in the South, but when we do, it arrives in a flash and catches us by surprise—an instant whiteout. Although it doesn't leave much behind, just a few inches can be more treacherous than a few feet. People think they can still drive, yet most have never seen snow in their lives. Traffic snarls, cars slide into ditches, school buses spin out and trucks jackknife.

Sean was on I-40, just west of Hazen, Arkansas. He was coming back from Little Rock loaded for California just like I'd told him. Staring through the snow, he did not know that a truck, miles ahead of him, had jackknifed and slid into the median, leaving the trailer across the left lane. Tragically, the driver had fled rather than put out flares that could have alerted oncoming vehicles. Sean saw the wreck seconds too late. He tried to stop but skidded into the truck. The load of plywood he was hauling slid into the driver's side of the cab and crushed him.

It was everything I'd been seeing in my dreams, except it wasn't me.

The moment I heard he was dead, life stopped. Trucks, marriage, God, dreams, bankruptcy, family, prophecy, business... and Sean. Days later, when I could finally think again, after accident reports and towing and phone calls to Sean's friends and family, I relived our final day together. The morning he picked up the truck, we had shared coffee at the house. I felt guilty that I'd had not talked to him about his walk with God. I felt guilty about everything. A depression settled on me like a lead blanket.

Trucking is a tight community. We all know each other. We all fight each other. We all help each other. People knew that my truck had been totaled and rebuilt. The erroneous conclusion they came to was that it had been deficient somehow and that this had caused the accident. As with most things in the court of public opinion, it was the accusations that held sway over the truth. My reputation was ruined.

Yet that is not what bothered me the most. I knew something no one else knew, not even Susan. But I had to function, so I shoved it deep within.

There was a lot to do. Insurance, police filings and an eventual lawsuit involving five lawyers. We sued the trucking company whose truck jackknifed. Paul's estate sued them too. The bank that held the title to the truck had a lawyer in the game. Everybody sued everybody. It was not enough that my friend was dead. Now I had to fight for my life in court. It took a long time to work its way through the bowels of the judicial system.

In the meantime, I hid from everyone. I was out of the trucking business but still needing money, so I went into tree trimming. Suspended sixty feet in the air, topping a tree that could just as easily rip off my head, became my place of solace. It seemed fitting, somehow. It would have been easier just to cut them down, but people still saw value in trying to restore them. I didn't see value in anything anymore.

The driver who jackknifed was eventually proven to be negligent. He was driving too fast, and when he jackknifed, afraid of being hit, he ran instead of putting out flares. Turns out he had good reason to run. His logbook was a mess. He was out of hours and still driving. I don't know if they ever tested him but I suspect he was drugged up something fierce.

The settlement from the accident covered our bills. We were finally out of debt and out of business. It was my exodus from trucking, paid for through my friend's life.

With the lawsuits over, I knew it was time to face a mile marker on my road of destiny. I chose a time when I knew traffic would be light, and I drove to Hazen, Arkansas, to stand witness at the very spot on I-40 where Sean lost his life.

I knew the place well.

1978

Three years before I got saved, I knew I was called to serve God. I just didn't know what it was. Funny how people say God can't look upon sin. Oh yeah? I couldn't get him to leave me alone no matter how hard I sinned.

Life was good. We were making bank. I'd been drinking for two weeks straight at a hunting camp my friends and I shared, and I'd just won $23,000 playing poker. Not bad for a drunk. Not bad at all. I imagined Susan's face when I walked through the door. She'd take a deep breath to launch her interrogation—a two-week bender was a long time, even for me—and PLUNK! Twenty-three large would hit the kitchen table.

No more questions, Honey? I didn't think so.

Of course, no plan is foolproof, and this fool spent a lifetime proving it.

That night in camp, I knew the end was coming. I was seeing double, the stars above me were spinning, and when I closed my eyes, the trees screamed my name. I was due to pass out at any moment. Being November, there was a chill in the air, but I was fueled up like an alcohol heater. So, I stripped down to my long johns and succumbed to oblivion on a log outside the cabin. The money I'd won lay strewn across the ground, tens and twenties scatted among the leaves, still bearing the sweat of the men who'd lost them.

It was in this esteemed state of human evolution that my cousin found me a few hours later. He'd driven from Wheatly searching for me. The message he brought shook me into consciousness like a bucket of ice water.

"Clay, you gotta get to the hospital right quick. They just took Susan. She went into labor. She's in a bad way."

When I heard "Susan," my heart turned to stone. My wife was seven months pregnant with our second child. It was too soon. I had to get to Little Rock... fast. I was too drunk to drive but not sober enough to care.

It was an hour to the hospital as I folded time and space, planets rushing past me, unnamed convictions surfacing. I knew there was a God. Knew it plain as day. And not just any god, but one who could do things. Right now, I needed something done, something big. Like the businessman I was, I began to negotiate, if that's what it could be called.

God, please save my wife. Please save my baby. Please God. I know you're up there. And I'm down here. And right now, I'm in a hell of a mess.

I got to the hospital at 2 a.m. The screech of my tires startled the emergency room attendant. I bolted from the truck and rushed toward the doors. I was covered in dirt, unshaven for weeks, and smelled like a bar toilet. He tried to stop me but I blew past him. The damn fool followed me.

"Sir, sir! You can't park there. Sir! That's the ambulance loading zone. Sir..."

"Susan Nash. WHERE IS SHE?" I screamed as my hands found his throat.

"Security!" he croaked.

"Where is *SUSAN NASH*?"

A nurse came running.

"You Mister Nash? This way, quickly."

I got to the room and found a couple of doctors learning over Susan. Tubes ran from her tiny arms. A stupid machine kept going blip...blip...blip. I wanted to smash it. Never much of an imposing presence until she got good and angry, Susan seemed swallowed by the hospital bed. Her eyes fluttered open and she mouthed a feeble "Hey, Clay."

I grabbed Doc Eshelman by the shoulders.

"What's the deal, Doc? How is she? Where's the baby?"

"Come outside, Clay."

"Susan, I'll be right back darling."

She nodded feebly.

In the sterile hallway, Doc Eshelman gave it to me straight.

"She's better, Clay. She's a fighter. We've got her blood pressure stabilized. I want to keep her overnight for observation. But I believe she's gonna be OK."

I fought back tears.

"And the baby?"

"Baby's gonna be fine, Clay. Nothing to worry about. You can spend a few minutes with Susan, then she's gotta rest."

My heart in a puddle, I went back to my wife, held her hand for as long as they'd let me, then told her that I was going home to check on Dawn, our oldest, and that I'd back in the morning. She squeezed my fingers. I felt her bones, small and delicate, over soft skin. The sweat on her palms said *come back soon*.

"Hang in there, Darling. Let me take care of a few things at home. Then I can give you all you need. Just wait for me."

"I don't think I'm going anywhere soon," she said with a weak smile.

Back home, I gathered some clothes, made arrangements with the neighbors to keep Dawn a little longer, and started to walk out the door when the phone rang. It was Doc Eshelman again.

"Clay, I'm sorry. You'd better not waste any time getting back here. Susan took a turn. We're doing all we can for her and the baby."

The phone went dead.

I was in my truck and tearing up I-40 again, closing the gap between Wheatly and Little Rock, cursing myself for ever leaving Susan's bedside. Apparently, my negotiating with God had done little more than tick him off. I cried my heart out as the mile markers flew by like a picket fence. Both hands on the wheel, I shook uncontrollably. It was time to double down.

What's it gonna take, God? What do you want from me? I'll do anything. Absolutely anything. I'll give to the church. You name it, I'll give to it. Just say the word, Lord.

God, please keep her alive. I need her, God. I know I've not been the best husband. Who is? Well, I'm not.

What do you want from me? What do I have that you could possibly want?

And in that moment, I knew.

God...I hear you. I've been hearing you. Alright...I'll preach. You want me to be a preacher? OK, I'll give it to you. Now, please save her, God. Just...please...save her.

My second violent entrance for the evening was more spectacular than the first. This time, though, nobody was foolish enough to stand between me and my bride.

The nurse filled me in as I ran to the room. Susan was fading and might not survive. The baby was coming and its viability was questionable. There was nothing I could do but sign release forms and wait. My hand shook so badly, I could only make a scrawl.

An hour later, Doc Eshelman came around the corner wiping his hands.

"She's gonna be alright, Clay. The baby's fine — premature, but she should be OK. You have a daughter."

That's when I couldn't hold it in any longer. The weight of the early morning's trauma broke me. I cried like a baby. The nurse got me some coffee and led me to a quiet room where I could gather myself.

I had to wait several hours to see Susan, but our new daughter Diane lay sleeping in the bassinet on the other side of the nursery glass. She was tiny, pink and wrinkled like a piglet. She had more tubes in her than Susan. A skull cap covered her tiny head and a miniature oxygen mask obscured her face, but I was sure she recognized me. I stared for the longest time.

So, this is what a miracle looks like, eh, God?

I remembered the promise I made a few hours ago, one I had no idea how to fulfill — another newborn rising with a life of its own and looking to me to provide. A scripture I'd learned in one of my rare church visits escaped from my heart. *"Wake up, sleeper, rise from the dead, and Christ will shine on you."*

I breathed this word into my baby girl fighting for her life on the other side of the glass. The hand of God was on me. I still didn't know much, but this I knew: God saved my family that night, and he would lead us on.

1985

Standing on I-40, I felt the wind and listened for my friend's voice.

I had driven like a wild man that night in 1978 and had lived. From that moment, a steady conviction had come over my life. It took another four years to lead me to the altar of salvation, but in that time, I had all but eliminated drinking and gambling and stopped cheating on Susan all together.

Now, three years after salvation, I knew God wanted something more. I just didn't know what. Well, that's not exactly true. We all know what God wants... in some sense. If we didn't, what would there be to run from?

What no one but God and I knew, however, was that at the very place on I-40 where Sean's accident occurred, seven years prior, I had cried out my surrender to God as I raced to the hospital, committing my life to ministry before I was even saved, all the while begging for the lives of Susan and Diane.

They lived. I lived. Sean died.

Standing on the gray highway, I wept for my friend. A semi blasted past. In that moment of agony, I searched the heart of God for answers. They were slow in coming.

I felt there had been an assignment against my life, but that through obedience to God and the fear from the dreams, I had been spared. Yet how could I reconcile the death of my friend with the birth of my ministry? I couldn't. Instead, I stood at the mile marker, the junction between life and death, and resolved to spend the rest of my days earning what my friend's life had afforded me.

The Lord wanted my attention and he got it. The trucks were gone, the business was gone, and all that mattered in the world was waiting for me at home. The choice was clear...at least to me. I could preach and go broke or continue to work and pay our bills. I knew this was the end of full-time business, but entering full-time ministry seemed like financial ruin. Ironically, wasn't that what my efforts to date had been trying to avoid? And now what? I'd lost nearly everything and one of my closest friends was killed doing what I was afraid to do any longer.

I couldn't escape it—Sean had died in my place.

With nothing to keep me from crossing into that silvery light, I entered a new dimension of being, a transformation long in coming. When the hands are ripped from the clock, it's time to meet the clockmaker. He finally had me where he wanted me.

We had so much further to go.

EPILOGUE

IN THE YEARS SINCE THAT FATEFUL DAY on the pavement gray, I have made good on my promise to God — essentially letting God make good on his promises to me, my family and all of humanity.

Susan and I were married on April 6, 1973, and as of this writing, have been married for forty-seven years. We have three children: Dawn, Dean and Diane, three living grandchildren and one with the Lord.

Since giving my heart to Christ, I have worked as a church planter and leader, including pioneering churches in Brinkley and Pocahontas, Arkansas and Dyersburg, Tennessee, where I pastored for fifteen years.

I was ordained as a Prophet by Rick Godwin on December 4, 1990, and earned a Doctorate in Theology from North Carolina College of Theology. It was a lot tougher than hauling rice to California.

I've traveled extensively overseas, ministering and establishing Bible colleges in Eastern Europe, working in Montego Bay, Jamaica, with Christ For the Nations. I've also worked with Dr. Lobick Ministries in Ziare, Africa, and ministered on the Navaho Indian Reservation.

In 2004, we moved to Southhaven, Mississippi, where we started Citygate Community Church. The church remains our home base as we travel throughout the world building the Kingdom of God.

We are also active in Network Ekklesia International (NEI), a relational network of ministries led by Dutch Sheets. My desire is to see the Church function as the Ekklesia, legislating Heaven's will into the world and raising up strong men and women to be leaders. If I could sum up my definition of a leader, it would be this:

> _A leader is someone who can take a group of people somewhere they don't want to go and cause them to discover that they have a purpose there._

Many more stories of my life can be found in my two books: _Activating the Prophetic_, and _Relational Authority-Authentic Leadership_. Both are available on Amazon or from our church: CityGate

Clay Nash

LAST CALL

DECADES AFTER MY SALVATION, I found myself at the funeral of a close friend from my hometown. Standing in the crowd with her back toward me was a tall blonde lady. I recognized her instantly and felt a strange elixir of joy and tragic loss.

It's all in the past, Clay. You're forgiven.

Still... it wasn't.

Yes, I'd been forgiven... and more. I'd been restored. Yet I had to face her — no, I had to face what I'd done — and this wasn't going to be easy. She had filled out a bit, as we all had. We were getting older. I supposed that should have made it easier. It didn't.

"Nikki?" I asked in a faltering voice.

She turned abruptly, surprise on her face.

"Clay! Clay Nash! How are you?"

"I'm fine, Nikki."

"I hear you're a minister now. That's wonderful."

My shame seared me deeply, and yet I couldn't see the slightest trace of malice in those wise, sweet eyes that still sparkled like forget-me-nots in a country pond.

Time to make amends, Nash.

"Nikki, I don't know how to say this, but I owe you an apology."

"Now Clay, listen. That was a long time ago, and we've both grown up since then. Sometimes we do things and we don't think about the consequences. You didn't break up our marriage. Jeff and I had our time. It just didn't work out. We were all so young."

In that moment, I realized what made me want her all those years ago. It was the same thing that drew me to Susan, something I craved but could not attain... not on my own. Nikki had a sense of honor and the purity that came from it.

"No, Nikki. I'm not talking about the night before the wedding. I'm talking about the Holiday Inn... after your divorce. I was wrong to even suggest it. Not showing up that night was the worst thing I could have done at a time when you were your most vulnerable. I hurt you, Nikki. I'm so sorry. I've never been the friend you thought I was. I lied to you, lied to Jeff, lied to Susan and tried to lie to God. I'm so sorry. Please forgive me."

She stared at me, obviously confused, and then to my wonderment, a smile started at the corners of her eyes and spread down her face until a light chuckle escaped her lips.

"You mean.... Clay Nash! You didn't show up either?"

ABOUT THE AUTHOR

JIM BRYSON HAS BEEN WRITING AND EDITING for over twenty years. His work can be found in the books of many prominent servants of God. His greatest joy, however, is writing people's stories, the stories of their lives.

We are living history. Preserving our stories grants future generations the benefit of all we have experienced. Forgetting our stories means they flow back into the ocean and return to the clouds.

I've seen things you people wouldn't believe.
Attack ships on fire off the shoulder of Orion.
I watched C-beams glitter in the dark
Near the Tannhäuser Gate.
All those moments will be lost in time
Like tears in rain.
Time to die.

Rutger Hauer

Made in the USA
Monee, IL
17 October 2020

45410185R00095